MARK HAMPTON

ON DECORATING

MARK HAMPTON

ON DECORATING

Written and Illustrated by Mark Hampton

Edited by Elaine Greene

CONDÉ NAST BOOKS RANDOM HOUSE NEW YORK

 Published in the United States by Random House, Inc., New York, and simultaneously in Canada by Random House of Canada Limited, Toronto. Most of the essays and illustrations in this work were originally published in *House and Garden*.

Library of Congress Cataloging-in-Publication Data

Hampton, Mark.
Mark Hampton on Decorating.
1. Interior decoration. I. Title
NK2110.H25 1989 747.213 89-860
ISBN 0-394-57987-9

PROJECT STAFF
For Condé Nast Books
Jane J. Fisher, *Director*
Lorraine Davis, *Editorial Director*
Jill Cohen, *Special Consultant*
Ellen Maria Bruzelius, *Direct Marketing Manager*
Kristine E. Smith, *Advertising/Promotion Manager*
Mary Ellen Kelly, *Fulfillment Manager*
Diane Pesce, *Composition*
Peter Bakker, *Color Control and Print Production*

Produced in association with Media Projects, Incorporated
Carter Smith, *Executive Editor*
Toni Rachiele, *Managing Editor*
Judith Tropea, *Project Editor*
Ann Harakawa, *Designer*

Manufactured in the United States of America

98765432

First Edition

In the spring of 1984, Lou Gropp, editor in chief of *House & Garden* for seven golden years, called and asked me to lunch. At the table with him when I arrived for our meeting was Denise Otis, a *House & Garden* editor and a friend of mine for nearly twenty years. The purpose of our lunch was to discuss whether I would be willing to write a monthly column on decorating. The idea was fantastic and wonderful to me and I will forever be indebted to Lou and Denise for starting me on the path that led to this book.

After a lot of fits and starts the columns began to appear. My wife was a constant source of support and inspiration as I struggled with what seemed like a return to homework and term papers. Carter Burden, whose taste and judgment I always admire, encouraged me to keep at it when I thought my ideas were drying up; and Elaine Greene, my editor at *House & Garden* and after, provided the steady guidance that made the whole process possible.

Mark Hampton On Decorating is made up of versions of most of the columns that appeared in the magazine over a three-year period along with nine new chapters that I wrote specifically for the book. The marvelous members of my office staff have given me the same invaluable help with this endeavor that they give in everything I do. And finally I am grateful to all the people of the past and present who designed and decorated and lived in the rooms that have inspired me all of my life.

CONTENTS

For Duane, Kate, and Alexa

INTRODUCTION

For forty years I have been looking at houses, thinking about them, drawing them, and daydreaming about them. The most important page in my third-grade workbook was devoted to a large color photograph of the Supper Room in the Governor's Palace at Colonial Williamsburg with its ravishing eighteenth-century Chinese wallpaper—wallpaper that was recently removed because it was no longer considered authentic enough. I saw the paper again in 1989 in the London shop of the dealer who purchased it from Colonial Williamsburg and I thought, as I often do, about how durable the decorative arts are.

Fortunately for me, both my parents loved furniture and houses. Wherever we went, there was a running critical commentary on the houses we passed. From my father I inherited the ability to draw, and to this day my mother has a keen eye for the beautiful. Her wonderful taste has been a continuous thread in my life. She allowed my mania for furniture to flourish through countless visits to antique shops. When I was thirteen my father permitted me to take over our basement to strip and refinish the old walnut inside shutters I had bought for the windows of my tiny room. They were my most prized possession until I got a car, and from the moment I installed them I considered myself a decorator.

We all know that interior decoration is seen by many as a frivolous career full of ruffles and flourishes and preposterous fashion statements. Yet to transform the bleak and the barren into welcoming places where one can live seems to me an important and worthwhile goal in life. Sometimes this transformation can stun the eye, sometimes simply gladden it, but these are not frivolous pursuits.

In an era when there is increasing despair over the inhumanity of the world around us, the concerns of decorating rather than seeming vain and irrelevant provide for me a wonderful refuge. This work has to do with people and beauty and the timeless activities of domestic life. At least our private worlds can reward us with peace and pleasure.

Colors

THE INCOMPARABLE REDS

*When I decorated this red
library—a small room
in a New York City apartment
overlooking the East River—
the walls were covered with linen
velvet, that rich and indestructible
material, and I put my favorite kind
of sisal on the floor.
The mantel is Louis XVI and the
French armchair is somewhat
younger. Reflected in the mirror is
a Modigliani that belonged to the
owner's grandmother.*

Everyone loves red—it is the happiest of colors. We all grew up surrounded by red things: toys of all sorts, wagons, bicycles; the list is very long. You don't think little boys would want to be firemen if fire engines were battleship gray instead of gorgeous red, do you? As the years go by, we continue to be surrounded by the familiar cheerfulness of red possessions and red clothing from coats to neckties. Red is a symbol of easy playfulness and it broadcasts vigor. The world of advertising knows this and is filled with red, both as a packaging color and in typography. Half the magazine covers are dominated by red, and then there are national flags, Santa Claus's suit, and Christmas decorations. In nature red fruits and flowers always seem to be the heartiest.

The ability to communicate mood is a characteristic of many colors, and red, I think, has more connotations than any other. These connotations have a great influence on personal taste in interior decoration. There are some strong prejudices against red in rooms. Some people with red-wagon memories may think bright red is a color for children's rooms. Others consider it a color best confined to public spaces: the carpet in the first-class lounge at an airport or the lobbies of some big hotel chain. Another turn of mind might find red entirely too ecclesiastical for domestic use. Visions of the minister's study or a Victorian vicarage or—even more extreme—of being in church. Oddly enough, the red that appears to be a sacred color to many people can have the opposite, profane implication when used differently. Crimson flocked wallpaper, for example, is synonymous with saloons and brothels.

Finally there is the most deeply rooted of all color prejudices against red and that is its historical association with royalty: red velvet and ermine

The red I love almost better than any other is a deep, soft Venetian red.

(purple is Roman), like the bedroom of Josephine at Malmaison. The history of red and royalty is amazing. As a child, I found it simply unbelievable that Louis XIV could have taken the time and trouble to worry about the scarlet heels of his shoes, much less be concerned with preventing others from having heels of the same color. And aren't throne rooms always red? If you go through some palaces, especially those in Austria, *every single room* seems to be done up in red. The bias against regal red is sometimes a distaste for those hopelessly rich and ambitious magnates of the last century who aped the aristocratic worlds they didn't belong to, making red interiors a symbol of everything wrong with late-nineteenth-century decoration.

So there is a problem. People who disdain red for interior decoration do not usually think it is an ugly color. To them it is an unusable color. But that has changed a lot in the past couple of decades, and the marvelous possibilities of red in the color schemes of houses seems to me to be more and more appreciated. Because red is such a strong color and tends to dominate, it is important to map out its use if you intend to use a lot of it. And using a lot of red is what we are talking about.

To begin with, red is a terrific color for entrance halls. There are a number of fairly clear reasons for this. Even if you are one of those people who cannot relax in an atmosphere of strong color, passing through a brilliantly decorated hallway can be very pleasant. Another reason I love red halls is the (usual) absence of windows, which often makes hallways very dark, and dark rooms are wonderful when they are painted red. A lot of people tend to think you should try to lighten up a dark space with light paint. Well, the way to lighten up a dark space is with electricity. If you simply paint a gloomy room a light color, you usually end up with a dim gray room, whereas if you paint a dark space a rich lush red, its darkness can take on a shadowy inviting warmth. Darkness itself isn't bad.

A red entrance hall also makes a good, strong central focus from which other colors can radiate. Red goes with an enormous number of other colors and it often exists in the printed carpets and materials that you might be using elsewhere. Demonstrating the adaptability of red is one of the most famous red rooms of recent times, which isn't actually red at all. Two of the walls are white and the other two are red and green and black printed cotton. The client was Diana Vreeland, who commissioned Billy Baldwin to do it many years ago. It is the embodiment of red as a color that can tolerate many other supposedly warring shades of itself in close company. Every possible kind of red flower and object just settles right in and looks completely at home. Another fashion goddess, Elsa Schiaparelli, had a room in Paris forty years ago that combined scarlet, claret, Chinese red, and cranberry red in a pleasantly bizarre way, cozy yet bold. Red is, after all, the color that means bravery.

If a red entrance hall doesn't appeal to you, how about a red dining room, in the coral range, which goes from lobster to melon? Coral red is undoubtedly a splendid color for a dining room. Flowers and porcelain, in addition to food colors, go so well with this kind of red. If your porcelain requires a pinker red, that group includes numberless shades that are equally lovely with flowers and linens and candlelight.

And now we come to perhaps the most fertile area for using red in the entire house: the library. All the decorative elements that are traditionally associated with libraries—books, old needlework, brass, and leather (think of all the stage sets you have seen)—are enhanced by many shades of red. The walls could be red with white woodwork and bookcases, and the insides of the

Coral is a splendid color for dining rooms. Flowers and porcelain, in addition to food, go well with this kind of red.

bookcases could be painted the red of the walls. On the other hand, the entire room, trim and all, could be painted red. If you are very fortunate, you might possess mahogany bookcases to stand against red walls. Or if you have natural wood paneling, you can bring in red curtains and quite a bit of red upholstery. Old leather blends beautifully with any number of red tones. Sporting pictures are superb on red walls or hung in the vicinity of red. And Oriental carpets are often seen at their best with a lot of red to complement them.

By the way, if you have a great fondness for a particular type of Oriental rug and have not yet found the one you want (or can afford), it is very easy and reliable to go ahead and plan the room around some future carpet of a particular sort. The dyes of such rugs, although full of natural variations, remain constant within the general tonal range of the individual type—Ushak, Tabriz, Sultanabad, and Kirman, to name a few examples. I have often painted and installed rooms for people who love Heriz carpets but who don't have the one they want. When the right one eventually turns up, it invariably fits in with the brick reds and blues and oyster whites selected in anticipation. In one illustration, claret red velvet and an ancient leather Chesterfield sofa are seen on an Agra carpet. I cannot remember ever seeing an Agra carpet that would not go with claret reds.

The red that I love almost better than any other and that is perfect for libraries or living rooms or any areas where red seems right is a deep, soft Venetian red or Pompeian red or whatever you want to call it. This warm terra-cotta red of old frescoes and Chinese lacquers goes more beautifully with the disparate elements of decoration than any other color. It is an easygoing background for books, pictures, needlework, Oriental porcelain, and lacquer of all sorts. It is also ravishing with any gilt bronze or gold leaf.

Particular reds create particular identifiable atmospheres. There is a kind of rusty, oxblood paint—was it *really* once made with the blood of the ox?—that can be counted on to convey a Colonial, New England, Shaker message. To this earthy red add a little homespun and some indigo blue and you can't miss, if an Early American mood is what you want.

Cerise is as formal as oxblood red is informal. For that broad range of Empire, Duncan Phyfe, and Classical Revival, no other color is as expressive as this brilliant cherry red, especially if you use a lot of gold trimmings. The Red Room at the White House is the operative case in point.

Our own dining room in Manhattan has walls glazed in two reds by the decorative painter Pat Cutaneo. Over the 18th-century English table, a Dutch still life hangs from a brass picture rail.

cerise is as formal as oxblood is informal.

In Christian Dior's Paris house, which he decorated with the help of Georges Geffroy, the claret red of the velvet used extensively in the sitting room was borrowed from the Agra rug. Facing the fireplace is a worn, typically English Chesterfield sofa in saddle tan leather.

Choosing a red is one thing, achieving it is another. I am always fascinated by the properties of certain colors that make them impossible to realize in some media and easy in others. Reds are *very* varied. You can produce a Chinese red, for instance, equally easily in straight paint or in a glaze. The same thing can be said of Venetian red. Deep rosy reds, however, often require glazing if you want to paint them on a wall. If they are attempted in straight paint, they become overly dark and muddy and lifeless; they do not work when they are opaque. Glazes, by comparison, are transparent, and when applied over the opaque undercoat, they create a subtle, soft, lively appearance.

Where is red not good? It's an interesting question and the two rooms that come to mind are kitchens and bedrooms. I have a friend who thought she wanted a red bedroom and realized she had never seen one. As an experiment, she painted one wall red—the wall opposite the bed. After waking up to it for a few days, she saw clearly that a red bedroom was not going to work. The reason for this (and it applies to kitchens as well) is that red is not a good color with the atmosphere of morning, whether one is thinking of the delicate light or of the relative fragility of people beginning their day.

Though it is not a good morning color, one can surely say that red is the very best nighttime color. In the glow of sunset or the last embers in the fireplace, with candles burning and a bunch of red flowers against a deep red wall, whether you are alone with a book or entertaining friends, the warmth and coziness of a red room are incomparable.

A RETURN TO PEACH
AND YELLOW

In the past twenty-five years or so, we have seen a lot more yellow and peach in decorating than we used to. Thank heaven these glowing and useful colors are back in the palette. I wish color were an area of design immune to passing fancies and prejudices, but some of our colors inevitably do slip in and out of fashion.

For years yellows and peaches were not deemed important colors. Even when I was a child, forty years ago, yellow was considered undignified and lacking in richness. Its more sedate cousin, gold, was the color one used for significant rooms. Yellow was thought of as suitable for children's rooms or kitchens. In the book on eighteenth-century decoration that John Cornforth wrote with John Fowler, yellow is described as having been unpopular for walls because it did not go well with the gold-leaf picture frames that filled nearly every room. That is a perfect example of a silly prejudice. We all know now that gold leaf and yellow look great together. The most beautiful yellow room from the eighteenth century that I know of (there aren't many, and I guess there never were) is the gorgeous yellow room at the Amalienburg, near Munich, and by God, the splendid stucco work is silver leaf instead of gold!

The problem with peach is even more serious. For ages it was thought to be a color fit only for ladies' underwear. It simply wasn't used. Now, however, all of this nonsense is over, and if anything, we're running the risk of being bored by too much peach and yellow. Especially when either one is used with lime green, or worse, when all three are combined. How many handsome old country clubs have we seen absolutely ruined by those insipid, summery combinations? But that is not the point of this discussion. Both yellow and peach have remarkable properties of flexibility and neutrality that make them suitable for dozens of uses. Paradoxically, they can be soft and subtle or strong, with enough of a jolt to suit the most adventuresome extremist.

I suppose the most thrilling yellow room I had ever seen, until I visited the Amalienburg, was the famous London drawing room of Nancy Lancaster, of Colefax & Fowler fame. Tom Parr, a partner in the firm, took my wife and me to see it when we were on our honeymoon twenty-five years ago, and it was breathtaking. The room itself is enormous, with a very tall ceiling in the form of a barrel vault. It had been the studio of Sir Jeffry Wyatville, the great nineteenth-century architect. On one long wall, there are three tall windows, the center one of which is in a deep bay. On the opposite wall is a large center fireplace, and at each end are tall double doors. The walls were painted and varnished to a high gloss. I have heard the color described in many different ways, from butter yellow to the color of a banana peel. It seemed to me to be neither of those colors but simply pure, brilliant yellow. Not greeny or lemony and not browny or goldy. Just the essence of yellow.

Mrs. Lancaster's curtains were unlined silk taffeta of exactly the same color, trimmed at the top with lots of cords and tassels, looped and swagged. The large pieces of furniture were covered in shades of off-white that went with the background of the old Axminster carpet. The small pieces were covered in a well-known Colefax chintz that is covered with clusters of roses on a background that appears to be greenish because of its tiny pattern of shamrocks. There is no yellow in the chintz, and there was no yellow anywhere else. There was, however, a lot of gold leaf and a lot of antique-white paint plus natural wood tones. It was spectacular in the sun, and glowingly lovely on gloomy days. The purpose of the color was to create a strong, exciting background against which all the colors of wood, gilding, carpets, flowers, and so on could stand out yet be harmonious.

At the same time that this room was decorated, around thirty years ago, the brilliant Mr. Fowler was also crusading for peach, another of his favorite colors. In the Mediterranean world, yellow and peach are commonly used for exteriors. In the cloud-covered world of England, these colors take on a warming usefulness in interiors. John Fowler loved paint that was dragged and stippled, and with these techniques and the old-fashioned painters that he had to work with, he used peachy tones in every shade from melon to shrimp to rich coral. Even now I find that solid peach paint does not work well except in the palest tones, otherwise it becomes heavy and dull, resembling pancake make-up rather than possessing the clear, lush qualities that can make it enormously appealing.

I can't imagine not being able to use one of these colors.

What makes peach and its related tones so useful and so fascinating is their ability to mix with other colors. If you study porcelains, you'll often notice how beautifully pinks and rosy tones go with peach. Blues and greens (even the dreaded lime green) fit in perfectly, and the range of white, off-whites, and creams is unlimited. What we often fail to notice, though, is the lovely effect of old, faded tones when used against peach. Perhaps that is why glazed peach is better than solid peach. Glazed peach is softer, and more acceptable with antique painted surfaces.

Still, many people don't like that faded look. Billy Baldwin differed entirely from his contemporaries at Colefax & Fowler in that he liked spit and polish and none of that old shabby-looking stuff that characterizes so many patrician English interiors. Mr. Baldwin's woodwork was usually crisp white or

In redecorating the historic Lincoln Room in Blair House in 1988, I used a yellow self stripe for the walls and window, yellow damask for the chairs, and a reproduction of an 1820 woven carpet in yellow, gold, and green.

painted to match the walls, and his glazes were fresh and clean. In a famous New York apartment of his own in Amster Yard, he went through one phase of yellow silk curtains, chaste Louis XVI furniture covered in yellow satin to match, yellow walls, and a highly polished bare floor of dark brown parquet. The whole room was strong. On one wall was a Matisse drawing in black ink, emphasizing the bold, sharp look of the room.

Between the extremes of Mrs. Lancaster's room with all of its old faded elements placed against brilliant shiny yellow and Mr. Baldwin's room of crisp yellow and white accented with black and dark brown wood lies a middle range of decorative possibilities in which yellow is equally at home. The rooms that come to mind are best illustrated by the yellow schemes of another famous decorator from the recent past, Eleanor McMillen Brown of McMillen Inc. For the twenty years that I have known her (and for a lot longer than that), her drawing room on East 57th Street in New York City has had plain, flat yellow walls with elaborate Directoire-style pilasters and moldings. The dark oak floors are strewn with clipped white goatskin rugs.

Her furniture is covered in shades of yellow beginning in a tone deeper than the wall color and ending in a shade that is lighter, almost ivory. The curtains are yellow. The accents, however, are brilliant lacquer red, primarily in the form of an elaborately shaped Venetian secretary with gold japanned decorations. Mrs. Brown's favorite flower, the red anemone, is usually to be seen in great bunches, and there is even a painting of them by Raoul Dufy. The chairs are Louis XVI, and still in their original white paint, which is flaky and discolored but lovely and somehow still fresh. The tables are polished mahogany. Crisper than Mrs. Lancaster's room, but mellower than Mr. Baldwin's, this setting proves what a neutral color yellow can be. It is sunny by day and glowing and easy to light at night. And I must mention that candlelight in a yellow room is sensational.

Although less neutral than yellow (is it because it is further from the pure neutrality of white?), peach walls are certainly a marvelous solution to the problems that confront those of us who are tired of beige or white. You could make a case for the proposition that peach or some related shade of it will go with absolutely any other color. And there are no limits to the places in which peach or some related shade of it can be used. The great Gothic gallery around the interior courtyard at Wilton House in Wiltshire has lovely peach walls with off-white trim and a stone floor. The wall color is oddly perfect with the medieval architecture. We've all seen dozens of peach rooms with chintz and light frothy-colored upholstery. Many, if not most, Oriental carpets are superb with peach in the background. The same is true for most needlework carpets. Bedrooms are suited to peachy colors. Dining rooms, with their still lifes of flowers, wine, and food, always look great with any shade of this inviting color. Bathrooms are warm and soothing painted in peach tones. What better color for any place where bare skin is a factor?

So it seems that far from being too childish, or too feminine, or too informal, peach and yellow should be considered as basic colors for a host of decorating needs. Tudor, Georgian, Mediterranean, contemporary, or Early American—regardless of architectural style or of personal preferences, I can't imagine not being able to use one of these colors. Some people don't like this one or that one, but I've never met anyone who disliked *both* of them.

THE VERSATILITY OF GREEN

Born in Idaho, Van Day Truex divided his adult life between New York and Paris as a designer and educator. A man of enormous influence, he was head of the Parsons School of Design and design director of Tiffany & Co. Van Truex's New York apartment, seen here, was a color laboratory for him. This is its green incarnation in the forties where the many shades of one hue had a catalytic effect upon one another. His prophetic sense of style can also be seen in his fondness for Regency furniture long before the present boom began.

The first professionally decorated room I ever saw was in 1947, in, of all things, a house in the country in Indiana. It was such a shock to me that I sat and pulled the fringe off one of the pillows (probably the first time I ever saw fringe on a pillow, too) and got a spanking the minute we got home. But this isn't about discipline and punishment. It's about the color green. The walls of this room were blacky green and everything else was white. The carpet was white cotton. The upholstery was white something or other, as were the curtains and the partially wrecked pillows. The woodwork was white, and the pictures had white painted frames. There was an enormous mirror over the sofa. It sounds too simple for words, but it was terrific. You mustn't forget that Dorothy Draper had been busy at The Drake hotel in Chicago sticking white plaster Rococo sconces and console tables on dark green walls all over the place. It was a definite look. And although it is always difficult to know who had which idea first, Mrs. Draper must surely be given the credit for convincing many people that very deep green walls were a good idea.

At about the same time, Billy Baldwin's sitting room in Amster Yard was being painted what he called "magnolia leaf green." It was a room built around mellow, aged tones—a Caen stone chimney over which hung a Rococo mirror framed in faded gilt, a Korean lacquer screen in shades of black, gold, and sienna, and a muted Samarkand carpet. The woodwork was dark green like the walls. The upholstery and curtains were the same dark green. The absence of white is noteworthy.

Then, also at the same time, there was the work of Van Day Truex on East 75th Street. This remarkable apartment was a color laboratory for one of

Blue-and-white porcelain looks wonderful against any green.

the most influential teachers of design of this century. First, it was all blue, then it was all red. Eventually it was all green. During the latter period, the walls were dark green, but less blue than the shade favored by Mrs. Draper. The color had a slightly mossier tone that welcomed lots of other shades of green, a thing to remember when you are choosing any color: will it be at ease with versions of the same color? In any case, Van's room had upholstery in an acid tone that would become one of the flagship colors of the fifties. The Bessarabian carpet contained several other shades of green along with black and rosy tones. Green porcelain and accessories of every shade of green and even vases of rhododendron leaves rounded out a nearly complete range of one color. Used in such a single-minded way, a color begins to play off on itself to the extent that virtually *anything* of the color in question becomes possessed of a decorative power that it would otherwise lack.

George Stacey, another gigantic figure of decorating in America, used dark green as a basic, almost neutral color. His New York living room was another of those one-color rooms against which good furniture and objects stood out in a stylized way without appearing cold or too studied. The various shades of green were warm and natural—less pompous than, say, red, and less chilling than blue—but rich in color and depth, and it is this basic quality of being richly colorful without seeming overpowering that makes the color green so interesting.

Another Stacey trademark was the mixture of coarse yellow, rich brown, tomato red, and strong, baize green. As in cooking, recipes for mixing colors can often be tinkered with, but some ingredients are less flexible than others. In George Stacey's great mixture, the color green is the one that cannot be excluded.

Yet many people say they do not like the color. I cannot tell you how often women say to me, "My husband hates green." What happened? Does it have to do with the courtiers of the Middle Ages who attached an emotion to every color? If so, what a pity that green was the color of envy, because it seems never to have lived it down. Of course, there are shades of colors that have terrible reputations, and I'm afraid the green category has a few of the most detested ones. Chartreuse is a beautiful color whose very names makes most people gag. (I suppose the worst color name, one which is always said with a wrinkled nose, is "puce." Most people seem to think it is a sickly green, when in fact it is a purplish brown.) There is no question about it, words attach a significance to colors that has nothing to do with the colors themselves. Poison green is another example. It was a great fad in the fifties, that fad-filled decade, and now it is the punk paradigm of good taste. *House & Garden* called it Bitter Green. It appeared everywhere—in clothes, in packaging, in commercial design, and certainly in decorating. Now, it's rare.

I still have the photographs of a beautiful house in Palm Beach that Valerian Rybar decorated in the early sixties. Practically the entire house is based on one color scheme—turquoise blue, white, and lime green. The Tilletts, famous for their hand-printed materials, printed up a series in complex variations of these three colors, and the result was a perfect, tropical, oceanside house.

Another shade that seems to be out of favor is the clear, light green that Robert Adam used again and again. Its main problem might be that superintendents love to use it for the walls of basement corridors. Combined with a lot of frothy white plasterwork and shiny mahogany, it is a marvelous background for practically any color mixture. Then there is Wedgwood green and its first cousin, Williamsburg green. Most people seem to associate these colors with blue-haired dowagers, but as with *all* colors, stereotypes are usually way off the mark. My favorite William Pahlmann room, again from the forties, had as its centerpiece an enormous sixteen-fold Coromandel screen. With it,

The Green Room at the
White House is part of a great
suite of state reception rooms
which have been redecorated
many times over the years.
The walls are now green moiré
matched by silk curtains, and the
furnishings are fine Federal period
pieces. The present mantelpiece
and chandelier were installed in
1904 by McKim, Mead & White.
This watercolor, which I did
for the 1983 Christmas card of
President and Mrs. Reagan,
is reprinted with their kind
permission.

Pahlmann used his traditional mixture of furniture styles, a good bit of mirror, even mirrored furniture, and everything that could be a color was just one shade of Wedgwood green. Even the floor was carpeted in that shade. It was far from being stuffy and would have suited Carole Lombard far better than it would have suited Queen Mary.

Charles de Beistegui, whose dazzling taste has had such a grip on so many people for decades, used green with great boldness in all of his houses. The example that stands out most in my memory is a sitting room at the Château de Groussay, not far from Versailles, where M. de Beistegui tried his hand at practically every known style in the history of French decoration. The room is large and square with a double-height ceiling. The furniture and architectural details are in the style of the seventeenth century. The floor and the oversize chimney are black, gray, and white marble. The walls of this room are a strong olive green, another shade that is often considered treacherous. The lovely antidote to this deep, rather ponderous shade of green is a profusion (Groussay is a profusely decorated house) of blue-and-white delft. Instead of a baseboard, there is a double row of bordered delft tiles. Even the inside of the fireplace is lined with blue-and-white tile. The effect of the green and the delft is brilliantly vivid and decorative. Blue-and-white porcelain and earthenware look wonderful, in fact, against almost any shade of green.

The opposite of the rather country effect of blue-and-white porcelain combined with green walls is the traditional luxury and drama of green used with a lot of gilding. Surely one of the most glamourous and beautiful rooms on earth is the vast white-and-gold Louis XV drawing room in the house of Hubert de Givenchy in Paris. First of all it is a correct room architecturally, unlike so many rooms that are doctored up with paneling and never really look like eighteenth-century French rooms. The paneling is white with gilt decorations of a superb quality and color. The furniture within the room is all of the period

31

you can use dark green as a basic, almost neutral color.

with the exception of a few upholstered pieces. A couple of things are off-white and there is some antique needlework. Everything else, however, is green. There are lots of different types of materials used, but they are all green and of a deep shade. What's more, this long, airy salon is entered through a much smaller although equally high sitting room with walls covered in deep green velvet, so you go from one dominantly green atmosphere into a white-and-gold one where green is the only color and the background is one of total lightness. Against these two very compatible backgrounds—one dark and one light—furniture and objects of the greatest beauty appear at their absolute best.

I have heard a dictum about the use of green that astonishes me because it is so wrong. It is said that in rooms looking out on the greens of nature one should avoid using the color green. It sounds well thought out but it is nonsense. Green is incredibly neutral. I recently finished a house in the Connecticut countryside in which all the rooms look out on wide lawns or stands of lovely old trees. The living room has French windows that greatly increase the effect of the views. The materials used are all in shades of sky blue, off-white, and soft, rosy pink. There are chintz curtains at the windows and chintz on two or three pieces of furniture and the walls are glazed a very pale lettuce green. All of the blues and pinks exist in the chintz, and of course the leaves of the flowers—roses, morning glories, and pansies—are green. But there is no plain green material, and in fact nothing else in the room is that actual shade of green. It is simply the background. Whatever the season, it is a color that leads the eye naturally and happily out to the sky and the landscape beyond. Inside, pictures, objects, and furniture all look wonderful against this soft, fresh backdrop.

The San Francisco apartment of Mr. and Mrs. Prentis Hale, which I decorated in the early eighties, has a drawing room saturated with green: green linen velvet walls, green silk taffeta curtains, green marbleized woodwork, green damask upholstery. The greens are glorious with the Hales' notable collection of 18th-century gilt furniture.

The weirdest example of the mixing powers of green I can think of is a room that used to exist in the house of Rose Cumming. Her back sitting room was painted and glazed and varnished a sort of deep, bright grass green. There were no curtains, and in the bay of the wide window sat a huge purple satin sofa. The carpet was antique Chinese in typical shades of blue, gold, and oyster white, and in the room stood a set of scarlet lacquer chairs in the Queen Anne style. I know this sounds like a giant hoax, but it was a fabulous room and almost impossible to fathom. Color is impossible to fathom. There is so much talk about it, but, finally, we have to see for ourselves. The real way to understand any color is to spend a lot of time looking, and when you think of it, green is one of the most pervasive colors in nature and in art. Whether or not it is predominant in decorating, it has an ability to settle in with practically any other color.

WHAT DEEP COLORS DO

George Stacey, one of the great colorists of American decoration, designed this deep blue room for Vincent Astor in the late forties. All the moldings are the blue of the walls. The mixture of furniture styles displays the freedom with which American design is identified: Louis XV mantelpiece, Venetian mirror, Georgian tables, Victorian needlework rug, and two stools Stacey designed in the fully upholstered 17th-century style.

For years the entire Victorian era was considered to have been dark and heavy—two pejorative words that linger even though we have rediscovered the charms of Victorian taste. The antidark bias deprives many people of the pleasures of having a rich, cozy dark room. Or a sleek, dramatic dark room. Or a cool, quiet dark room. Dark rooms come, you see, in a number of varieties.

Gloominess is one of the chief problems with deep-colored interiors and they can also be overdramatic and extreme, but these are certainly easy problems to remedy. Gloominess is most often the result of a lack of decoration: pretty lamps, personal objects. Too much drama is usually the result, to put it baldly, of vulgar taste. If you see shiny navy walls, lots of mirror, and a deep-purple satin banquette with lights along the bottom, blame the taste, not the darkness.

Now for the good points. One of the most positive attributes of deep-colored rooms, one not known to many people, is that they look larger than they are. The reason for this is that the boundaries of the space become lost in shadow; the walls and corners seem to recede. This effect is most noticeable in small hallways, studies, and libraries. Mood is another factor. There is a hushed, peaceful quality about dark rooms that is very agreeable. Dark rooms also offer another advantage: They are fabulous backgrounds for either cluttered or minimal decoration. Rooms with light and medium tones cannot do this unless everything is kept in the same color value. One last benefit, and a very significant one, is the wonderful way dark rooms continue looking clean.

When my wife and I added a large living room to our Long Island house, we painted the walls a dark, dark brown—a color that is cool and shady in summer, warm and cozy in winter. The flower-color palette is derived from the famous La Portugaise striped chintz on the chair in front of the bookcase built to my design by Greg Gurfein.

If the decorating schemes in the rest of your house run to chintz and colors considered rather feminine, a deep-toned room gives you an easy way to break the routine. Dark rooms nearly always look more masculine than feminine. I don't mean that the only way to create a dark masculine room is to concentrate on leather chairs, guns, and decoys. Nor do I mean that all chintzes are necessarily feminine. There are some marvelous exotic chintzes with dark and especially black backgrounds that are masculine as well as cozy. I remember photographs of a great Georgian room paneled with dark-stained pine which was decorated over thirty years ago by the firm of Smyth, Urquhart & Marckwald. The most important elements of the design scheme, in addition to the paneling, were a large, dark Coromandel screen, an Oriental carpet, and a mammoth baggy sofa covered in black-background chintz. It was the ideal man's room.

In the contemporary high-tech household, a deep-colored room would be the obvious location for the television set, especially one with a gigantic screen. If the room is to function as a screening center, you could make the space even darker by painting the ceiling the same color as the walls. I should warn you, however, that this might produce a theatrical or nightclub effect. Most screening rooms do remind me of bars in hotels.

There is nothing new or faddish about walls in deep colors. Think of all the dark oak and walnut paneling in English and European houses. Although there is certainly a question about the original hue of such fifteenth- and sixteenth-century rooms, they grew darker over the years in any case. And the Victorians in their zealous revivals of earlier styles often interpreted paneling in dark browns. Most of us would agree that such walls are rich and dignified, and men who think they dislike dark walls are frequently crazy about brown paneling.

The most daring of all deep colors is, of course, black. Sir Edwin Lutyens, the brilliant English architect and idol of today's Postmodern movement, whose work spanned a half century from the 1890s to his death in 1944, loved black although he shunned showy decoration. (For instance, he and his mentor, Gertrude Jekyll, the immortal garden designer, disliked cut flowers in a house. Imagine this—they told their clients to leave them where they were growing!) Lutyens chose black walls, which were usually shiny, primarily for their ability to emphasize architectural details. In his own drawing room in a lovely Georgian house in Bloomsbury Square, the walls were black, the floors were stained green, and the curtains were yellow.

At Folly Farm, a house he designed in Berkshire, Lutyens created a high barrel-vaulted hall with abundant architectural woodwork and plasterwork painted white. Again the walls were black. At one end a Chinese Chippendale balcony was painted lacquer red. He often used shiny black walls in hallways. The choice is excellent. A strong dark hallway can separate and punctuate the tamer spaces leading off in various directions.

There is a practical side to shiny dark walls. It is good to keep in mind that when using deep tones in flat or even matte finishes the paint scuffs very easily. Light colors do not scuff, but on a dark surface even one's elbow gently brushing by can leave a cloudy mark. The finish should at least be a low-gloss paint. If the plaster is wonderfully smooth, then you can attempt a high gloss. Although varnish causes colors to yellow slightly, many deep shades benefit from this top coat—just the way oil paintings look better after a coat of varnish.

About forty years ago Dorothy Draper decorated a drawing room at the Carlyle Hotel in New York and painted its double-height walls charcoal gray. The elaborate Georgian-style details were painted white. There was a large Dutch marquetry cupboard with a bombé base. There were dark portraits in old giltwood frames, a pale blue damask sofa, gold damask curtains, and Mrs. Draper's signature rose-covered chintz chairs. It was beautiful then and would be beautiful now. That cannot be said about all of forties decorating.

At the same time Billy Baldwin's living room sported magnolia-leaf green walls as a background for antique carpets and Oriental lacquer, and George Stacey covered the walls of the Gracie Square drawing room of Vincent Astor in a blue deeper than lapis but the same hue. The Astor curtains were off-white. The furniture was covered in several materials—deep green, a rich cerise red, and, combining all these tones, a chintz with a white ground, pink and red flowers, and green leaves. The room was multicolored, but the intense blue dominated everything.

George Stacey, whose superb work for the Paleys, the Harrimans, and even Ava Gardner was classical in inspiration and boldly stylish in details, has a New York living room that is to this day an example of his daring way with color. The room is filled with French and English furniture, and his palette is made up entirely of four elements: black, lacquer red, lettuce green, and gilt bronze. If all these lively components were new, the effect might be harsh, but the balance between newness and antiquity is so perfect that the effect is completely harmonious—bright, chic, stylish, quiet, calm.

William Pahlman was for many years a leading influence on American decorating, and in the forties and fifties he, too, was an enthusiastic promotor of deep color—sometimes in schemes carried out in monochrome, sometimes using a variety of hues and tones. One room that stands out in my memory had slate gray walls, gilt Louis XVI chairs in cerulean blue leather, and a big cabinet covered with snakeskin. Above the cabinet hung prints and drawings framed and matted in a variety of ways. The slate walls had a calming effect on an otherwise hyperactive group of elements typical of forties Moderne.

About twenty years ago Mrs. Henry Parish radically changed her drawing room from cream and soft green to a scheme that consisted of shiny Coca-Cola brown lacquer walls with flame-colored silk taffeta curtains and swags. The furniture was covered in off-whites and a strong yellow chintz that included the flame red. All the same paintings and antique pieces remained, but the atmosphere had completely changed. A few years later, when she moved to a new apartment on Fifth Avenue, Mrs. Parish made the walls deep eggplant color, again shiny, and covered the furniture partly in the creamy off-white she loves and partly in pink and mauve tones using silk painted by Alan Campbell. The curtains were mauve cotton edged in, of all things, a ruched piping of hot geranium red. All the colors in the room, whether pastel or strong, appeared to be more vivid against their dark background.

Paint, wallpaper, and wall upholstery materials, in addition to paneling in wood tones, are all possibilities for dark wall coverings. The range is so wide that something can be found for virtually any decorative scheme in any conceivable house or apartment. I don't mean to imply that everyone must have a deep-colored room, but I do think that a bias against dark colors is foolish. One of the most important things to remember about taste is that while we are striving to refine it, we should try at the same time to broaden our point of view. Greater appreciation can only enhance our visual lives, and that enhancement is the point of decoration after all.

THE QUALITY OF WHITE

For something most people do not count as a color, white and all the tones of offwhite provide a variety of rich decorative effects that no bona fide pigmented hue does. Historically there have been many beautiful whitewashed rooms in peasant cottages and great palaces, but they were rooms where whiteness was a background. In modern times, white along with the pale neutral range that I call no-color has developed into a real point of view which still exists as a bold, stylish way to decorate a room and seems to be gaining in popularity after a few years of being eclipsed by the nostalgia for lush colorful fin de siècle decorating.

I don't know when the first intentionally designed no-color room appeared. It would be interesting to know whether it evolved or was the result of someone's brainstorm. It could certainly be argued that after the nineteenth century, color-free interiors were bound to appear. Looking at many photographs and watercolors from a hundred years ago, one has the feeling that white had almost ceased to exist, and with the whiteness went all the air as well. Often upon entering shops that specialize in old upholstered furniture, I feel an intense need to escape from the dusty atmosphere all that decaying velour and fringe create. The early no-color designers must have felt the same way, and although we now know that any style of decoration can be interpreted in a no-color way, ninety years ago the idea seemed very modern. Charles Rennie Mackintosh, that pivotal figure in the history of modern design, created rooms in Scotland that changed the way architects and designers have looked at things ever since. From Vienna to Chicago, his influence was tremendous. Josef Hoffmann and Frank Lloyd Wright might not have existed as we know them had it not been for Mackintosh. In contrast to rooms that were formal, rich, and dark, Mackintosh's interiors were informal, rather

A rich range of decorative effects can be achieved with no color at all.

Everything is slipcovered and starchy and washable in Albert Hadley's whitewashed barn in Maine. Fabrics are cotton and linen; colors are whites and beiges. Even the carved wood stag's head has been whitewashed.

cottagey, and light. This quality of lightness extended to the actual construction of the rooms and everything in them, ruling out the use of the gilding and heavy carving so prevalent then.

Another seminal influence at the time—and one who had a similar effect to that of Mackintosh—was James McNeill Whistler. All you have to do is glance at one of Whistler's monochromatic portraits with hints of Japonesque decoration in the background and you can immediately grasp his extraordinary gift for style and atmosphere. When compared with other portraits of the same period, his are simply revolutionary. In a very good essay on modern interior design by Edgar Kaufmann Jr., published in 1953 by the Museum of Modern Art, Whistler's influence on the decorative arts is given enormous emphasis and the argument is very convincing.

By the 1920s there were full-fledged examples of creamy white rooms that have become landmarks in the history of interior decoration. One of the most famous was the London drawing room Syrie Maugham created for herself in the late twenties. Everything in the room was pale and creamy except for the piano, which was hidden by a low parchment-covered screen. Behind it stood another screen made up of thirty-odd six-inch-wide mirror panels framed with chromium-plated metal. Can you imagine making a screen like that today? Mrs. Maugham's big boxy sofas were slipcovered in off-white and trimmed with coarse fringe. The geometric carpet was by Marion Dorn, the brilliant carpet designer who at the end of her career worked in this country. The low lacquered coffee table was the sort that we associate with Jean-Michel Frank. The flowers were off-white as always. The effect that this room must have had on visitors stumbling in from the soot of London before coal fires were banned was no doubt fantastic. With it an entire school of interior decoration was born.

One must not forget Paris. Jean-Michel Frank was a more serious influence than Mrs. Maugham. His furniture designs are still very much a part of present-day decoration. The objects he commissioned from Diego Giacometti are more sought after and valuable than ever. He was a near genius, and the room he created at 11, place des États-Unis in Paris for the Vicomte and Vicomtesse de Noailles in the late twenties was another one of those landmarks of design which gain in beauty and appeal as time goes by. The walls of this high-ceilinged room were covered in large panels of parchment. The enormous double doors were sheathed in bronze and allowed to darken. All of the upholstered furniture was again huge and boxy and off-white. The curtains were plain and of the same tone. It was certainly very stylized. When I saw it in 1970, forty years after its creation, this remarkable room was still an exciting and beautiful example of decoration, in spite of time and change. The blank walls had become covered with great French paintings by twentieth-century masters. Books and objects crowded tables that were originally bare. The furniture had funny-looking white cotton slipcovers. In short, everything that goes on in a house over a period of time and often ruins its decorative effect went on in this bold room without destroying its boldness. Colored paints and textiles *would* have destroyed it.

The exciting and extravagant rooms I've just described could perhaps be considered as just so much passé glamour—fine for Jean Harlow but not pertinent today. That isn't the point, although the dramatic aspect is definitely a strong one. The no-color philosophy is applicable in a broad range of decorating and can be practiced in widely divergent situations.

Take, for instance, two rooms created by Albert Hadley nearly twenty years apart, one in a barn in Maine and the other in a splendid New York apartment. The barn room had all the characteristics that make you want to turn every pretty old barn into a house. There were old rough beams and great open spaces. A tall window, reminiscent of an artist's studio (another fantasy mood I always love), provided light and a broad view over fields and woods, the sort of view barns are supposed to have. The floors, walls, and ceiling were different tones and textures of white and off-white. The upholstered furniture was covered in a pale cotton twill that was neither beige nor cream. A beautifully carved trophy of a stag's head with real antlers was whitewashed and hung over the mantel. A few pieces of furniture were painted white and others were left in natural straw or bamboo. Some fur pillows blended in with the naturalness of the accents. There were witty references to every possible twentieth-century phase of interior design. Living together in contented harmony were a 1950s standing lamp in chrome and steel, a Louis XVI bench covered in Dutch East Indies batik, Lucite tables, angular sofas like Syrie Maugham's and Jean-Michel Frank's, Regency bamboo, and even a calfskin rug. The aim was not to achieve a flashy opulence with calla lilies in goldfish bowls. It was to create a summery mood of carefree simplicity, lightness, and comfort in addition to an amusing stylishness based on a broad collection of furniture. The vehicle for this ambitious objective was the no-color scheme.

The goal in the handsome Park Avenue apartment was entirely different. Working with a certain amount of formality, a beautiful collection of old master drawings, and a broad range of very special eighteenth-century furniture, Albert Hadley utilized a no-color scheme to dispel the richness inherent in the possessions of the owner, substituting a softness and comfort more appropriate to our age without sacrificing any of the beauty that we all long for. The drawings by Van Dyck and Rubens look marvelous, the Louis XVI chairs in their original needlework are divine, and the golden Regency serpents wriggling up the legs of a console are frightening. All this complexity is displayed to perfection against a palomino background.

A further effect of this sort of pale luxury is the way in which it frames the views out the windows. The changes in light and color take on the clarity of an Ansel Adams photograph. The way off-white monochrome decorating provides a perfect foil for surrounding terraces and gardens is well illustrated by an enchanting Barbados house designed by the late scenic designer-turned-architect Oliver Messel. Its present charm is due both to the great taste and style of its owner and to Bunny Williams, who, under the tutelage of Albert Hadley and his partner, Sister Parish, has grasped the effectiveness of using a no-color scheme in direct juxtaposition to a ravishing tropical garden by the sea. In this case, however, the monochromatic scheme is not confined to a room or two. The entire house is decorated in varying shades of cream and off-white, with a constant repetition of an accent color that ranges from face powder to peachy pink. In the evening as the sun sets over the Caribbean, the distinction between ivory and peach becomes so blurred that it is nearly

off-white decorating is a perfect foil for surrounding terraces and gardens.

impossible to tell what color anything actually is. The orchids and lilies from the garden become the lightest, brightest tones in the rooms. Needless to say, the atmosphere is wonderful: peace and quiet without dullness.

The extraordinary aspect of these rooms is that they are all so different. Eschewing color doesn't reduce rooms to a state of sameness. On the contrary, it allows a host of elements to come into play. As a background for art and antiques, a no-color scheme is both subtle and dramatic. For a lover of gardens and landscape views, it provides a noninterfering middle ground through which the details of the outdoors are seen with special clarity. In the hectic and dirty confusion of city life, it offers a surprise combination of extravagant luxury and quietude. Architectural details, both modern and traditional, stand out in marvelous relief against an airy color-free backdrop. And if there's a family controversy over which colors to use, why not settle it by opting for no color at all? It would be a lot more satisfactory than tossing a coin and ending up with a color you don't like.

In Anne Bass's Fifth Avenue drawing room the only color is in the fine English Axminster carpet of the 1770s. The Georgian chairs have gessoed frames. Wall covering and upholstery materials are various off-white silks. Silvered iron torchère was made for Versailles.

45

Elements

FIREPLACES

It would be difficult to imagine a room with a fireplace in which it was not the dominant architectural focus. Where an original fireplace exists intact, chances are that the mantel design will also be the most elaborately developed stylistic feature of the room. To be sure, very ornate architecture can include lavish overdoors, cornices, and ceilings; the fireplace, however, is frequently the centerpiece, both figuratively and literally speaking. Where humbler building styles are concerned, the mantelpiece usually holds the position of most important or only important architectural element in the room. Often it is the trademark of the period.

Original mantels frequently do not exist in situ. There are a couple of easy explanations for this. First of all, mantelpieces are so pivotal in terms of design and style that replacing or remodeling them has always been an obvious way to update the background of a room. A new fireplace can completely alter a space. Also, because they are easily removed and relocated, many beautiful old fireplaces have been yanked out and sold for the embellishment of new buildings or for the improvement of existing rooms somewhere else. This brisk traffic in old mantels (I've even heard of mantelpieces being stolen from vacant buildings) occurs not only because they are easy to reinstall but also because they are loaded with architectural and decorative significance. The sculptural quality of some chimneypieces is fantastic. More important is the fact that the word *hearth*, and all it implies, is deeply rooted in our romantic thoughts about home. I hope I do not have to justify my conviction that nearly everyone prefers a room that has a fireplace in it to one that does not.

So here is this profoundly entrenched idea of a focal point to our rooms which I guess we'll just have to presume is a legacy from the caveman, who also expected to arrive home and find a fire waiting for him. And like us, I suppose the caveman wanted the principal seating group arranged around the fire.

The word hearth is deeply rooted in our romantic thoughts about home.

Although we may feel that a fireplace is required, we are not impelled to let our decorating style be dictated by it. I have illustrated the same mantel—a simple, mildly Neoclassical design in the style of Louis XVI executed in gray marble—in three different moods. In real life this fireplace adorns the sitting room of David Hicks's wonderful flat in London. The flat is in that splendid building called Albany, which consists of a grand Georgian town house to which the architect Henry Holland added two apartment-house wings in the early years of the nineteenth century. That's a whole story in itself, but suffice it to say that there are no apartments in the world quite like them.

David Hicks has treated his Albany fireplace in a completely personal way, a way that has in fact become a trademark of his style. With characteristic deftness he has arranged a small antique head, a red chalk drawing, a tiny thing of flowers, a dark glazed porcelain covered vase sitting on a marble base, a piece of Lowestoft, a carved gourd with vermeil mounts, and a Classical column and obelisk. That arrangement is liable to change at a moment's notice. A more permanent element of the chimney ensemble is the small self-portrait of Sir Joshua Reynolds that hangs on a sheet of mirror above the mantel. The combination of the informal, rather spontaneous still life and the more formal, static background of a portrait hung over an old mantelpiece has everything to recommend it. It is interesting and lovely to look at, yet it is not unnecessarily jarring; that is to say, it is not coy or annoyingly self-conscious.

The fact that it can easily be changed makes it fun for the owner and fun for the visitor. The problem with this sort of approach is that you have to have a knack for arranging still lifes. Some people have it and some people don't. If it suits your taste and you are capable of pulling it off, then do it your way. The need for this sort of competence applies to almost every aspect of the decorating of rooms and negates most other rules. (Too much of this competence might have a seriously negative effect on the interior decorating trade!)

It is conceivable that for a variety of reasons you would prefer to treat your Louis XVI fireplace in an entirely different way. Styles change, moods change, people's possessions change. In another illustration I have imagined the same mantel, but in the hands of someone who has another point of view. Instead of striving for a look of casualness that implies change and whim, this person wants the fireplace to be integrated into a design composed of all the various elements of a stylistic moment in time. The wall of the chimney breast is treated as a single entity. Above the mantel hangs a mirror in the mantel's style. Flanking the mirror are a pair of gilt-bronze sconces consistent with the whole scheme. The ornaments on the mantelshelf are equally Classical in spirit: a bust, a pair of porcelain flower holders, and a pair of urns, which could be crystal or porcelain. One thing should be pointed out about this sort of composition; all the objects should be of the highest quality you are capable of. David Hicks is famous for being able to combine objects of surprising but appealing disparity, including a disparity of quality and value. It is an unconventional gift. Where more conventional and traditional results are desired, I think a stricter attitude is necessary—not that traditional decorating shouldn't be fun. There are, however, rules that have to be taken into consideration the minute you embark on a project based on the correct interpretation of a style.

The third version of this fireplace addresses the problem of simultaneously desiring traditional decoration while wishing to be allowed a good deal of self-expression free from too many strict rules. In my opinion that dichotomy explains the popularity of rooms decorated in a sort of English style in which pictures, porcelains, and accessories of virtually any period can be mixed. The hypothetical fireplace in this last version is embellished with Oriental porcelain vases, an eighteenth-century clock, and an array of invitations, postcards, and perhaps a recent glowing report card or a drawing by the pretend owner's pretend nine-year-old. The wall of the chimney breast is hung with Regency brackets on which stand Staffordshire figures and an assortment of miniatures, all clustered around a central painting. Each and every one of these things could be from a different country and a different century and the effect might be more or less the same.

In each of these three treatments of the same fireplace there is an implied mood that should extend to the rest of the room. Not all mantel styles are as flexible as this one, but many of the most popular ones are—which accounts for their popularity. The limitless variety of Georgian and Colonial types is well known to everyone. They can be marble or wood. If wood, they can be painted or stripped. If painted, they can be dealt with in a correct historical sense or they can be tarted up with wild abandon, provided that's the

way you're headed. French mantels, especially smallish ones, are frequently graceful and lovely in rooms that lack scale, as Billy Baldwin and Sister Parish have demonstrated dozens of times. The interesting thing is that a French mantel can look great in a room that really doesn't have anything to do with French furniture, but an English mantel isn't quite so flexible. The most demanding area of all in the design of a mantel or in the selection of an old one is the problem of scale. Of all the criticisms I can think of that arise regarding fireplaces, errors of scale are the most common. Scale violations are generally those in which the height is off. A big tall grand Georgian fireplace made for a big tall grand room is neither convincing nor pleasing in a low-ceilinged room with dinky doors and details. The general rule, of course, is to adhere to historically proven proportions. What a simple rule—so often unheeded.

The subject of fire tools and fire screens occupies an inordinate amount of time with a lot of people. Neither tools nor screens should be very obtrusive, in my opinion. Little stands with little sets of tongs, pokers, and shovels hanging on them which are constantly being knocked over are not very appealing. A couple of useful tools, preferably old, standing around are good-looking and easy to deal with. There is a C-shaped brass thing called a jamb hook that screws into the wall or mantelpiece against which fire tools can rest. A nicely made brush or broom can lend a touch of simple handicraft, which is always attractive.

Screens are even more complicated, and the modern glass-fronted built-in whatchamacallits in the chimney opening drive me nuts. The safest screen is the freestanding spark guard that completely seals the opening with black wire mesh. Very plain folding screens are nice. Roll-down screens are fine—expensive, but fine. Then there are the curtains of mesh that draw to the sides. They aren't bad at all, but on a small opening they can take up an awful lot of room. Freestanding modern glass folding screens can be very chic, and antique ones, if you're lucky enough to find any, are pretty and unusual. But for the most part, the less fuss made over these prosaic accessories the better.

As in all discussions of decorating, the question of ugliness is always lurking around the corner, but I love fireplaces from practically every period. The Aesthetic Movement produced some examples of originality that are impossible to describe. If you are ever in Washington, go see Whistler's Peacock Room at the Freer Gallery—it's fantastic. Frank Lloyd Wright's cavelike stone chimneys are stupendous. Nineteenth-century mantels can be preposterously rich. Then there are those mountain lodges with fireplaces made of huge boulders, not to mention Renaissance Revival, Arts and Crafts inglenooks, the Vienna Secession. Fireplaces are keynotes of creativity in the history of decoration. Like nothing else in a house, they wrap up a wide variety of decorative and architectural needs and desires. Given this enormous significance, they deserve serious attention.

Reading across the top of these pages from left to right are three possible arrangements for the same Louis XVI-style mantelpiece, which actually exists in David Hicks's London flat. The first is Hicks's own deft, personal ensemble; the second could be a design by someone who wishes to integrate all the elements in one strict style; the third arrangement is both traditional and informal.

DRESSING THE WINDOWS

For some reason, critics of decoration are fond of aiming their barbs at curtains, making fun of the amount of design energy and client money that is usually required to deal with the whole window situation. (I am struggling to avoid using the term *window treatment*. If Nancy Milford disapproved of *drapes*, imagine what she would have thought of *window treatment*.) Decorating is a lot of fun; it is also a pretty serious business, and designing and making curtains is very important to the final result. It is certainly possible to make silly or wrong-looking curtains, and many otherwise sane rooms take on an embarrassingly overdressed look because of misguided or overly ambitious curtains. But avoiding the issue with a lot of Roman shades or vertical blinds won't work in many cases.

In most rooms, traditional as well as contemporary, nothing is more assertive from an architectural point of view than the windows. They are structural, after all, and unlike moldings and mantels, they are difficult to change. This is all the more true because they have an exterior as well as an interior role. Indeed, the houses that have been ruined by someone's tampering with the windows would provide material for a good-sized book. Even in a time when apartment-house windows are constantly being replaced, the shape and proportion of the new ones usually repeat that of the old. Think for a minute about the strong associations that come to mind in relation to various types of windows: tall French windows, small casement windows with leaded glass, floor-to-ceiling sliding glass windows, simple picture windows (usually with an air-conditioning unit coming out underneath), double-hung windows with twelve or sixteen panes. These different window types call to mind rather specific styles of architecture; unless something serious is going wrong, the big Georgian house does not have the picture window.

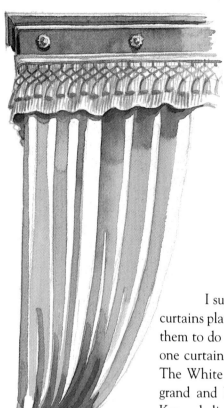

This is a detail of the curtains
in the Blair House Lincoln Room
(also seen on page 24) which
hang from a valance board
painted bronze green
and decorated with gilding.
The beautiful fringe was made in
Paris. I took the design from an
1820s house in England decorated
by Humphry and John Repton.

I suppose that because windows are so difficult to change and because curtains play such a large role in the decoration of a room, many people rely on them to do more than should really be expected. But certainly changing from one curtain style to another can completely alter the atmosphere of a room. The White House, to cite a familiar example, took on the atmosphere of a grand and beautiful private residence during the years President and Mrs. Kennedy lived there. The curtains in the Green Room were rather plain, with valances in the form of shaped pennants, made of the same watered silk as the walls. Later this same room took on the aspect of an American Federal historic room, primarily because of the curtains, which were made in a very strict and accurate way, with swags hanging from gilded cornices of molded wood and long wooden-tassel fringe on the panels.

Correctness in curtains has to do with many things. Suitability is one. Expensive, elaborate curtains look out of place in rooms with no real scale and no good furniture. Here is a bad example: Imagine fin de siècle curtains of the sort so popular now in claret-red velvet, perhaps, embossed in a damask pattern and trimmed with great fringes and tassels, with ruched Austrian shades underneath and perhaps a lace panel behind that. Imagine this in a nondescript room with a small white-painted cornice molding, a simple mantelpiece, plain floorboards with no borders, doors with ordinary hardware, and conventional upholstery. Even if one were to cover the good Lawson sofa in the same velvet, one would still not even have begun to live up to the curtains.

Here is another example of the windows and the curtains insisting on suitable furnishings: Imagine a room with lovely tall French windows curtained

The Great Swag Problem

Negative

If your ceiling is not high you have to deny yourself big swags, as the illustration, I hope, proves. There are other, more modest traditional solutions to the problem, which our American ancestors learned.

in a French way, the poles light French ones (not stocky Regency English poles) with rings and finials and crunchy taffeta curtains tied back with cords and tassels and passementerie rosettes. That room would then simply have to have some French furniture in it. That's all there is to it.

Another consideration is the appropriateness of the materials to the design. Pretentious valances and curtains look terrible if they are made of poor substitutes for rich fabrics. Just as gold radiator paint is not highly regarded as a substitute for gold leaf, so synthetics do not take the place of beautiful silks and cottons. Trimmings must also be considered. They can take months to make and can cost more than the material for the curtains themselves. If there is an economic question, simple designs finely executed in first-rate materials are surely superior to elaborate designs in second-rate materials.

Good scale is the designer's great ally, and it has everything to do with curtains. Rooms with high ceilings (ten feet or more) pose fewer problems than rooms with low ceilings. If the room and its furnishings have a prevailingly Georgian, English, Colonial (whatever you want to call it) style, and if the ceilings are high, you can do what you want, but some attempt should be made to follow the patterns of the past. There are endless guides that make it easy to determine the difference between the various eighteenth- and nineteenth-century curtain styles. Bookstores are full of works on decoration, many of them detailed studies of particular periods. Museums all over the country have period rooms with painstakingly reproduced curtains. Try asking the curator to allow a close look; I often do. This theoretical tall room, provided its windows have a strong verticality, can take on aspects of any traditional style. And if

In our living room in Manhattan the curtains are made in the so-called tableau style, drawn up by cords invisibly sewn on the back of the panels. By being tied back at a high point, the 18th-century-style curtains raise the apparent height of the windows.

you don't want to be confined to any particular period, simple curtains permit you to be contemporary or eclectic.

We don't hear much about eclecticism nowadays, but it is still a point of view that exists and should be dealt with. In rooms where French and English and contemporary (or Biedermeier or Italian) furniture are combined successfully, the background always seems to be rather spare or neutral. I remember the extraordinarily beautiful sixties rooms in Rome of the painter Cy Twombly: hard, bony rooms of plaster and stone over three hundred years old with huge modern paintings and some lavish Neoclassical furniture but no color to speak of anywhere, and the windows bare except for the usual indoor and outdoor shutters of a palazzo. The same rooms would have been totally different with the dark, heavy curtains typical of a century ago. They would have been different too with the gauzy Neoclassical drapery of a century and a half ago.

Perhaps I am sounding too dependent on historical precedents. There is certainly a lot of room for new interpretations. The most successful adaptation of a traditional curtain design to a contemporary setting hangs on a slender bronze or brass pole that is a wide U-shape in plan. On small rings, severely pleated curtains are attached without any heading whatsoever. This was the design of the Paris firm of Jansen a number of years ago and is now a permanent part of our vocabulary.

Actually, French curtains have a history of being plainer than their English counterparts (until the nineteenth century, of course). This is surely the result of the emphasis the French placed on paneling. Once again, documents provide the most interesting and illuminating sources of inspiration. Look at paintings by Boucher and Fragonard with billowing unlined curtains in the background, shoved behind the back of a chair or tossed over a folding screen. Such curtains don't have a rigidly confining design effect on a room. Any contemporary room would look marvelous with simple, unlined curtains made of some lovely silk. The great Tugendhat house designed in 1930 by Mies van der Rohe had, after all, great expanses of silk shantung curtains that were part of the richness achieved by combining marble, ebony paneling, and mirror-polished chrome.

If you don't have the height, a category into which most rooms fall, the news is not good. Discipline is required. It's like being on a perpetual diet. Big valances and swooping swags are out. An exception to this gloomy rule lies in the area of American Colonial curtains. With their genius for creating formality within tightly compressed spaces, our ancestors invented lovely buckram valances in many shapes that have a lightness and fineness of scale that is perfectly suited to the low ceilings and smallish windows of Colonial-style houses. Verticality is the key, however. Low, horizontal windows, I'm afraid, require very plain curtains. Fortunately the use of beautiful materials and careful workmanship elevate the simplest design.

When I think of curtains, the analogy that comes to mind is that of clothing. There are all these tiresome bits of advice dealing with personal adornment, how it all has to harmonize and interrelate. The same is true in the world of curtains. Whatever you may think you want hanging at your windows, it has to go with your room, your furniture, and your whole decorating style.

LAMPLIGHT

For twenty-five years no trip to London was complete without an afternoon at Geoffrey Bennison's shop in the Pimlico Road. Blue- and-white porcelain, old textiles, lacquer, and an eccentric collection of furniture were the trademarks of this brilliant, influential antiquarian-decorator. This vignette of his shop is illuminated by a lamp made from a Chinese vase—a lighting category with a long history and an undoubtedly bright future.

It seems to me that the act of leaving a lamp lighted on the hall table for those who have not yet returned for the night is rather like the ancients leaving lamps on the altars of their favorite deities. It is a warm, loving gesture and a welcoming sight to the one who is returning. Somehow, leaving a recessed ceiling light on doesn't quite evoke the same cozy feeling. Yet when I first began working in the decorating world in the early sixties, an awful reaction against table lamps was going on and everyone of a certain forward-looking point of view was frantically trying to eliminate the beautiful, useful, and time-honored lamp. Well, those days are over, for a while at least, and as is the case with all lighting (it never ceases to surprise me), the recent lampless look still exists while lamps of every known sort also continue to exist. The world of lighting is constantly expanding but it never contracts. The possibilities simply increase.

It is almost impossible for us to imagine the world without electricity. Whenever there is a power failure and we find ourselves surrounded by lighted candles, I always marvel at the grip darkness has over us. One of the basic elements of ancient lamp design is portability. Every little oil lamp made two thousand years ago had a handle so you could move that light from one dark place to another. "Lighting the way" was critically important, and the design and manufacture of the artifacts that provided the light took on a good deal of importance, too. Ancient Etruscan lamps, for example, were beautifully made and were a great source of pride to their owners.

Candles were in fact known in ancient history, but they did not become common in domestic use until after the Middle Ages. Because of their costliness, they were confined for centuries to religious use. They were made of tallow or wax, and in France there were two separate guilds for the two

For many of us, the most agreeable way to light a room is with table lamps.

different sorts of candles. When candles finally hit the domestic scene, they provided an outlet for decorative design that is profoundly felt to this day. The historical range of candlesticks and candelabra is vast and completely wonderful as a source of inspiration for modernists and traditionalists alike. The materials used in candlestick making are tremendously varied—wood, brass, pewter, bronze, silver, porcelain—just to name a few. There are not many useful, decorative articles that inspire such widespread creativity and variety, or that have traveled down through time with so much adaptability. The bouillotte lamp, for example, is a beautiful design usually consisting of three bronze candle branches and a painted tole shade. It was made to light a gaming table in the eighteenth century (the game was called bouillotte). It has, with the substitution of a couple of light bulbs, become an indispensable type of lamp right up to the present day, and I feel it is safe to say that it will never be out of favor.

In 1784, a Swiss inventor named Argand came up with a new kind of oil lamp that did not have the problem of making a lot of greasy smoke. It marked the beginning of another era of lighting, which, coupled with all those candlesticks, still has a great effect on the design of what we call lamps. Many of the shapes that became familiar as oil lamps were easily adapted to electricity a century later.

Another aspect of lamp design that is interesting to me is the fact that lamps are a remarkably clear indicator of the fashion of the times. They are, in an odd way, a fashion accessory—in fact, lamps can be thought of as the jewelry of interior decoration. They can be quite precious; they can be retired and brought back at a later date; they can be remounted. Or they can be given a new type of lampshade, and *presto*, they fit right in again. The subject of lampshades alone provides us with an indicator of time that can be as accurate in establishing the date of a room as counting the rings on the stump in dating a tree. How often an old photograph of a divine room is marred according to present-day standards of style (fickle and feeble though they may be) only by the funny, outmoded lampshades.

In the first twenty-five years or so of this century, rather elaborate (sometimes *very* elaborate) Chinese-style pagoda-shaped silk lampshades with frills and ruching and fringe were used on lamps made out of Chinese vases. Such vases, by the way, had been mounted as candelabra since the eighteenth century, so they were, by the time electricity came into domestic use, time-honored objects in the realm of lighting. These extreme Chinese lampshades eventually gave way to a more conservative shape, and for years, there was a commonly used lampshade with concave outlines that was a simplification of the overly designed pagoda shade. Later on in the forties and the fifties (oh, how I love to gripe about the fifties!) we saw the insistent and very ugly drum-shaped lampshades that still appear in motel rooms and other places of dubious decorative distinction. Then came the simple tapered shade whose shape can be more or less conventional. In the sixties, I remember loving the marvelously chic Paris apartment of Roger Vivier, and one of its outstanding features was the design of the lampshades, which were of an exaggerated coolie-hat shape, made of shiny opaque paper. They became the instant rage.

As we all know, lampshades can make or break a lamp. Just exactly what makes a good lampshade is, like taste itself, a difficult thing to define. However, there is always my favorite test, which is easy to apply: What has looked best for the longest period of time? Usually, if a design has consistently won out over the other entries in the race, then it is pretty good. And in lampshades, where proportions mean everything, unless your intention is to create an extreme shape, like that of M. Vivier, the most appealing lampshade is one that tapers, but not too radically. Its vertical measurement should exceed the top diameter, but not by an enormous amount. Steeply tapered shades, which have a top diameter that is a great deal smaller than both the bottom diameter and the vertical dimension, are usually best when used on rather small, spindly lamps, which means that the shades themselves are small. The larger the shade gets, the more difficult it is to scale it. These same loose principles of proportion apply to hexagonal and octagonal shades as well.

The materials that can be used for shades are numerous. Paper shades can be clean and strict looking, especially when the paper is opaque—either shiny or dull. Translucent paper, on the other hand, has a soft glowing quality when the light is on that is less hard than the opaque. If you have a clever painter, you can also glaze translucent paper shades, which results in an aged look whether the light is off or on. Opaque paper shades can be tinted for that matter, but it doesn't affect the quality of the light. Linen, cotton, and silk, whether pleated, shirred, or stretched tight, are beautiful and rich. Color tonality is terribly important, since dead white can be so glaring. Soft pink linings are loved by many but the pink must be a very subtle shade. The whole mystery of selecting a lampshade is largely solved if you are able to take the lamp with you to the place where the lampshades come from. Certainly the safest approach is to opt for the simplest design made in the best possible way.

In spite of the tendency of lamps to be rather trendy accessories, it is still undeniable that a good number of lamp types have remarkable durability. They are real classics. Here is a brief list: (1) The OK-to-fine Chinese or Japanese vase mounted as a lamp. (Note: if it is a good vase and has never been mounted before, do *not* drill a hole in the bottom of it. That little hole will ruin the value of your antique. The cord will be just fine dangling out of the top of the mounting.) (2) Gilt-bronze candlesticks mounted with a false candle and topped with a delicately scaled shade, which are lovely in pairs or used singly. (3) Bouillotte lamps, already described. (4) Crystal columns with gilt-bronze capitals, usually the bases for oil lamps that have lost the reservoir part of the mechanism, which makes very crisp and elegant lamps. (5) Different types of wooden candlesticks, Italian baroque as well as simple Georgian examples. (6) Battersea and other sorts of enamelware candlesticks. What's more, these various types of lamps all go together, which is part of the challenge.

Bunches of new lamps fresh off the assembly line, on the other hand, do not look very rich, and if you do not want a rich effect in the first place, then make your lamps out of simple earthenware vases, or old hand-blown glass bottles and jars, or severe terra-cotta or plaster shapes. The Diego Giacometti plaster lamps are yet another example of the persistence of great design. They hold the same charm now that they did fifty years ago. Another huge category of lamp-base types is the broad range of Empire and Regency partly dark and partly gilded candelabra that can look very grand but that can also look very hotel-lobby if you're not careful. And finally, although I know I have only scratched the surface, there are all the urns of the world that have been converted into lamps—wood, marble, porcelain, bronze, tole, and on and on. For those of us who adore Neoclassicism, urns are always welcome.

Twentieth-century design has added a number of well-known classics to the list of permanently available lamp types. The way a style can last is remarkable: The 1924 Rietveld table lamp is half a century older than the 1972 Tizio lamp by Richard Sapper, yet they could be used just a few feet away from each other or one could be used instead of the other. Their design inspiration is the general language of the Industrial Revolution, which has had such a profound impact on modernism. It is noteworthy that many of the starkly modern lamps of this genre create hot spots or pools of light rather than general, soft illumination, partly because they were intended to be used in

spaces that had a lot of ceiling light. This quality of casting sharp pinpoints of light only increases the sculptural feeling of the lamps themselves.

Within the realm of modern lighting, one must also consider the vast area of Art Nouveau and Art Deco lamps. Without being unappreciative of those periods, I do feel that Art Nouveau and Art Deco were such radical developments and so highly ornamented and stylized that they do not permit a very eclectic use of their artifacts. For example, Tiffany and Gallé and all the other art-glass lamps look out of place in most rooms. They are most commonly and most successfully used as collected objects, not as functional decoration.

When we are thinking about decoration, the fact remains that for many of us the most agreeable way to light a room is with table lamps. In addition to creating seductive pools of light of whatever intensity we desire, they provide us with a satisfying amount of decorating that is limitless in its variety. They can also be placed wherever we need them or want them. Rich and grand, arts-and-craftsy, redolent of some bygone era, or modern and strange—there are styles and designs that can fit in with any décor and suit any design sensibility. And the acquisition of a new lamp—unlike a track light—doesn't usually necessitate calling the electrician.

Three table-lamp classics from the left: an electrified gilt-bronze candlestick with a false candle, a Chinese vase mounted and wired, an 18th-century bouillotte in bronze with its original tole shade.

MIRRORS

In Rose Cumming's New York City brownstone the dark ground-floor dining room was decorated on all four sides with 18th-century Venetian mirrors in Rococo frames painted and silver-leafed. The glass was old and mottled, the squares were held together by tarnished rosettes. Between the mirror panels, the ancient-looking walls were soft gray. Repeatedly reflected in the mirrors was the overscale Louis XV chandelier burning its black candles.

People think all too often that mirrors are a little showy, perhaps a bit commercial and more appropriate in dress salons and nightclubs, or that they are too Baroque, too Rococo. The fact remains, however, that mirrors are both beautiful and useful. Their beauty is often over-shadowed by the richness of their frames but the silvery sparkle and the sense of illusion that they contribute to a space is certainly uplifting. Mirrors are also very durable. Like porcelain, they combine opposing characteristics of fragility and durability—a tantalizing dichotomy.

The word *mirror* probably comes from the Latin word meaning "to admire," and for many centuries the only mirrors in existence—whether of highly polished metal in ancient times or of glass backed with metal in medieval times—were small hand mirrors made expressly for the purpose of looking at oneself. Early in the sixteenth century a couple of very enterprising men from the island of Murano in the Republic of Venice obtained a license granting them the exclusive privilege of making mirrors. Theirs were glass, usually beveled, backed with a silver-colored amalgam, and large enough to hang on the wall. For the next 150 years, Venice monopolized the mirror trade in the Western world.

These early mirrors, highly prized and famous throughout Europe, were treated with the same care and attention that collectors gave their paintings. The estate of the French minister Colbert, who died in 1683, contained a Venetian mirror 46 by 26 inches valued at 8,016 livres. A painting by Raphael

This late 18th-century English mirror is a design that has been executed many, many times. Its stylized palm leaves, carved and gilded, form one of my favorite frames. There are many old ones and many copies in the world today.

in the same estate was valued at 3,000 livres. These mirrors were not intended for the guest powder room—they were major pieces of interior decoration. It is no wonder that Louis XIV's Hall of Mirrors was and is one of the world's most astonishing rooms. The idea of a room primarily decorated with mirrors was truly palatial. It is almost impossible to imagine the manufacture and shipment of all the mirrors of the seventeenth and eighteenth centuries. How on earth were they packed? Were there great, horse-drawn equivalents of today's eighteen wheelers piled to the skies with mirrors wrapped in hay, rumbling along the roads of England and the Continent? There must have been.

Perhaps the most familiar mirrored room, with the exception of the Hall of Mirrors at Versailles, is the round room in the Amalienburg, one of the Maisons de Plaisance in the park of the Nymphenburg Palace outside of Munich. Designed in the 1730s by Cuvilliés as a hunting lodge for the Electress Amalia, this little pavilion contains a suite of rooms of Rococo perfection. The most dazzling of these rooms is also called the Hall of Mirrors. The background of the paneling is pale blue. The carving, almost too ornate to believe, is silver leaf. And the panels themselves are completely filled with large panes of beveled mirror. The effect of the icy light combined with the extravagant design is preposterously rich.

Owing to the element of white metal in mirrors, they shed a light that is as cool as silver. Therefore, when combined with cool colors, mirrors can create a marvelously frosty effect. The room in the watercolor belonged to Rose Cumming. It was the dining room on the ground floor of her enchanting house across from The Museum of Modern Art on 53rd Street in New York. The room itself was low (ground floor, after all) and dimly lit by one bay window slightly below the level of the sidewalk and facing north. It was an unprepossessing room to say the least. The walls were paneled with painted Venetian moldings in which were set squares of very old, very discolored mirror. The squares were held in place by tarnished brass rosettes that had once been gilded. The moldings and the intervals of wall in between the panels of mirror were painted a soft gray with traces of polychromy. The floor was white marble with squares of black. The rest of the furnishings were varied to the point of incoherence; the background and Rose's taste held it together. Although everything was in a state of decay, the evenness of tone in the room was perfect, and because of the combination of faded mirror and shades of gray, there was a cloudy quality that can only be called ethereal—one of the lovely possibilities of mirrors.

The special qualities of fantasy that were second nature to Rose Cumming are not available to most of us. Neither are antique Venetian mirrored rooms, for that matter. But mirrors and their endless uses are certainly at the fingertips of all of us. One of the most practical uses of mirrors, in the past as well as now, is the creation of light on an otherwise gloomy wall or in a dark part of a room. Forgetting whatever else they reflect, it is important to remember that they throw light back into the room. The perfect example of this is the pier mirror, one of the first wall-hung types. Pier walls—walls between windows—are always cast in shadow as a result of the light passing through the windows to the other side of the room. By hanging long mirrors in these narrow spaces, the inevitable shadows are replaced by reflections of the side of the room where the light has come to rest. In this century, a new alternative has presented itself, and that is just to haul off and cover an entire wall with great sheets of clear mirror. That, naturally, creates both additional light and the illusion of doubled space. It is an even more effective trick when used in conjunction with some kind of view. The thing to remember, though, is to place the mirrors at a right angle to the wall with the view, not opposite it.

A Régence carved and gilded mirror hangs over the marble fireplace in the white drawing room at Estée Lauder's villa in Saint-Jean-Cap-Ferrat, which I decorated in the early seventies.

If you want to combine confusion with illusion, mirrored folding screens are marvelously decorative and whimsical. The most beautiful ones of all were made for Syrie Maugham and had sixteen or twenty panels seven inches wide edged in tiny frames of beveled glass. I once found one in a client's garage, where it had been packed away years before in plywood crates, about five panels to a crate. Assembled, the screen gave the effect of a row of giant prisms. What it would cost to make one of those screens today I couldn't even begin to imagine, but we all know that simpler versions can be fabulous.

Far from considering mirrors too showy or the least bit inappropriate for any kind of room, I think there are not many rooms that couldn't use one. One of my favorite rooms and a perfect example of just how far you can go is at Stratfield Saye, the home of the Dukes of Wellington. The room I love so is mid-Georgian with dark green architectural elements picked out in gold. The walls are covered in an early Victorian wallpaper festooned with gold swags and garlands, and there are lovely paintings against this rich background. But it is full of mirrors as well, and they are not parts of a large matching suite. There is a pair hanging on the window wall in their proper position as pier mirrors. There is another larger, grander one hanging over the fireplace. Finally, there is a second pair flanking the principal door to the room. With the windows and therefore the natural light confined to one wall, all these mirrors perform their many functions. They reflect the beauty before them, their frames provide decoration on their own, and they throw light back into the room. It seems to me that you could make a very strong argument in favor of mirrors not as a luxury but as a practical necessity.

DEEP COMFORT IN SEATING

For her current Fifth Avenue apartment Mrs. Henry Parish II interpreted a Victorian sofa for her living room. It is a beautifully curved piece with soft details; the tufting, the pleated corners of the skirt, the gathered arms. The richly swagged and fringed curtains that are always associated with Mrs. Parish are executed in the kind of clear color she is also known for. A patterned Axminster carpet is on the floor.

I think we would all agree that the sort of upholstered furniture that is sometimes called overstuffed is essential to comfort. Until about a hundred years ago, however, the majority of people had to do without it. From the seventeenth to the nineteenth centuries, odd bits of furniture upholstered in a way that more or less resembles some of our modern-day pieces crop up in various documents, but they are fairly rare. A well-known seventeenth-century sofa actually survives at Knole, the Tudor house in Kent that belongs to the Sackville-West family. It is covered in some ancient velvet, including the frame. It is hard to believe that this piece of furniture, so familiar to us today, was made a few years after the Pilgrims landed in Plymouth. There are a great number of paintings, drawings, and engravings that show fully upholstered banquettes or divans, usually in alcoves or niches, as in the 1750s Gothick gallery built by Horace Walpole at Strawberry Hill. Those pieces had no springs, which did not come into use until the 1830s (they were literally overstuffed), nor did they have beautifully carved frames like everything else in Walpole's room. There was no "show wood," as the English call it, because the divans were for sitting, not ornamentation.

By the second half of the nineteenth century, large houses were full of upholstered furniture, many in styles that have come straight down to us with hardly a change. I say large houses because big sofas and chairs first seem to have been used extensively in country houses in those huge rooms called halls—not halls as passageways but great rooms, near the front door, that were furnished with comfortable informal furniture. They were classless rooms where anyone could be received—children, dogs, bailiffs, farmers—and this casual association still clings to a lot of upholstered furniture, as does the masculine clubby aspect. One still hears people refer to large overstuffed chairs as club chairs.

I suppose it is natural that as life became more comfortable and informal, furniture suitable to this way of living would become more prevalent. But at the same time innumerable houses, even into this century, continued to have formal drawing rooms or parlors that contained no large upholstered pieces. These rooms, with their chairs and settees that stood on rather spindly legs, symbolize to us stiffness and discomfort. They possess a body language that says to the person standing at the threshold, "Come on in if you want to, but you're not going to be able to relax." Manners were stricter then. The reverse message, one that is inviting and promises comfort and pleasure, is communicated by the presence of generously scaled upholstery.

Not only do many of the sofa and chair designs that are popular today differ very little from those of eighty or ninety years ago, but there is a firm in London, the Howard Chair Company, that began as a chair maker in the 1820s and has been rolling along ever since. Their marvelous furniture made today looks just the way it did in *Country Life* photographs at the turn of the century. Some of the pieces have had to be scaled down a bit, but the outlines and proportions have been scrupulously preserved. New York firms, some of which stay in the same family from one generation to the next, manufacture many of these same styles, and they even continue to use some of the old-fashioned names that identify specific designs. The Bridgewater chair with its softly curved arm is known by that name everywhere. The Chesterfield, in addition to identifying a type of overcoat, means to most people a tufted sofa whose back and arms are the same height. The enormous Charles of London chair takes its name from a decorating firm that belonged to one of the Duveen brothers, who, it is said, was forbidden to use the family name by his aggressive brother Joseph, head of the family art business and eventually a lord. Tuxedo Park gave its name both to a dinner jacket and to a high-arm sofa style.

Many upholstery designs are evolutionary forms. The Knole sofa, for example, is derived from a high-back settee. The wings of the arms were brought forward and squared off, and pillowlike pads were sewn on. They had to be attached because the arms let down by means of a metal ratchet. The modern St. Thomas sofa, one of Billy Baldwin's favorites, is the contemporary descendant of this design. The reason the seat cushion extends under the padding of the arm is, I'm sure, that it developed out of the relationship of the seat to the arm on the Knole version. There are many more contemporary designs that are equally tenacious in their ability to remain in the staple diet of decoration and design. Most of them have some deep roots in the past.

Another approach to furniture history is to study it in relationship to decorators and architects. If you enjoy looking at photographs of McKim,

Mead & White houses as much as I do, you will be amused not only by their architectural details but also by the firm's persistent preference for certain upholstered furniture styles. One fascinating example is a low-slung and incredibly deep sofa with a tight seat and back, that is, no loose cushions. The seat height is literally one foot off the floor (most sofa seats are about fifteen to seventeen inches high). The beautiful casino built by Stanford White for the Astor family at Rhinebeck had these wonderful, funny-looking sofas around the indoor swimming pool. There were perfect for lolling in and conveyed that lazy message by their appearance alone.

In the far-ranging work of Elsie de Wolfe, one sees rather chaste ladylike sofas and chairs that were conceived by a woman whose chief love was lightly scaled, proper period furniture with carved frames. The upholstered pieces were intended simply to fulfill an almost neutral utilitarian role. Their decorative effect was negligible; they were there for comfort and unobtrusive necessity. Her great rival, Syrie Maugham, on the other hand, loved fanciful sofas and chairs that were plump and somewhat exaggerated. Often these pieces were tufted and done up with pleats and bows. It is perfectly clear that the one practitioner of the decorating trade put valuable furniture first and the other put decorative effects ahead of everything else; they each leaned toward the type of upholstered furniture that best suited her point of view. That is exactly the attitude we can and should adopt today, especially since it is possible to order up anything you want.

The modern St. Thomas sofa, seen here in a version made by the New York City upholsterer Guido De Angelis, can be viewed as a descendant of a 17th-century piece that survives in England.

Many of the most
popular sofa and
chair designs differ
very little from those
of eighty or ninety
years ago.

In Charles de Beistegui's Venetian Palazzo Labia, which I visited nearly thirty years ago, the great salon with its heroic tapestries, Savonnerie carpet, Murano glass chandelier, and Neoclassical stove contained the kind of traditional English sofa and chairs that are still standard in any upholsterer's showroom.

If you happen to possess a suite of beautifully carved Louis XVI chairs and want to achieve a formal atmosphere of richness and luxury, you will want to avoid big upholstered chairs and will limit yourself instead to a graceful sofa style that is neither too huge nor too masculine. It should be the type that allows you to use some fancy trim—perhaps cording in the seams and a base fringe. French upholstery styles (more than English and American) include designs that allow one to hang elaborate tassels from the ends of the arms and the backs. This type of upholstered furniture requires a pretty jazzy support system—everything should look rich. French upholstery also goes well with all the somewhat eccentric nineteenth-century decorative styles that are so popular now.

The Victorian explosion has been responsible for the revival of a lot of slightly cranky but marvelous-looking and very comfortable chairs. Their swooping backs and short eccentric legs add great style and an element of amusement to a room. The corresponding sofas seem less useful, often not made to stand against a wall. More up-to-date models, by means of fringe and tufting and ruching, can be modified to go with an odd assortment of the Victorian chairs many of us love.

I should point out that a decent upholstery workroom can achieve astonishing changes in the design of an existing wood frame that you already own. You cannot alter the basic shape of a frame, but you can add or eliminate rolled arms and backs; you can square off a chair that is too rounded or soften one that is too hard-edged. Backs can be raised or lowered. Why bother? Because it is often difficult, except in a large city, to find a source for frames, and it is far safer (and cheaper) to modify one than to start from scratch.

Contemporary rooms demand upholstery styles that harmonize with the art and the architecture and the general mood you are trying to achieve. For years I have watched people with a taste for contemporary styles needlessly rely on stiff-looking modernized upholstery that, even when comfortable, looks so hard and forbidding that no one in his right mind would ever sit on it. There are, however, many designs that are inviting and at the same time in harmony with modern architectural styles. The St. Thomas sofa is an example.

The current mania for Russian, Baltic, and Biedermeier styles poses a fresh set of challenges. Sofas in particular can be difficult to integrate with this stiff-looking northern European furniture. The problem is intensified in rooms where period settees are used. In these styles, the settee designs are a marvel of ingenuity and invention, but very often they are tall and high-backed. These proportions frequently make normal upholstered pieces placed nearby look as though they are standing in a hole. This is not a felicitous look, and ordinary upholstered pieces should be avoided.

It was not easy in the past to find upholstery manufacturers whose lines included much variety in design. In recent years, thank heaven, all that has changed, and people who decorate for themselves can now choose from a vast array of styles, both historic and new. As with all decorating decisions, it is helpful if one's taste is developed to the degree that most purchases have a way of becoming a part of a coherent whole. We all change though, and in the selection of upholstered furniture, you fortunately have the option of modifying it if you find that it has become outmoded. If you stick with styles that are to some extent rooted in the past, you can bring your sofas and chairs forward and backward in time as fashion dictates without throwing them away. One of the essentials is to find a good upholsterer. With his help, decorative miracles can be worked, and better still, you can be in complete control. Perhaps there should be a bumper sticker asking, "Have you hugged your upholsterer today?"

THE ENGAGING
SLIPPER CHAIR

Few pieces of legitimate furniture have the ability to make you smile. Odd bits of antlers and horns or elaborate wood carvings from the Black Forest do not qualify. The sort of furniture I have in mind is that fairly large category of charming and sometimes slightly funny-looking pieces known as slipper chairs. They can possess an amusing quality that belies their usefulness in almost any living room combined with almost any kind of antique or upholstered furniture.

The slipper chair is probably derived from the eighteenth-century French *chauffeuse*, a small chair on short legs made to draw up to the fire. Like its ancestor, the slipper chair is usually armless. Both chair types tend to have backs that are low in relation to other chairs, and their shapes are often fanciful. These fanciful shapes occurred from the start, probably because of the dwarf aspects of their scale—a normal-sized seat and only slightly narrowed back on seven-inch legs, for example—and because these were single chairs, unique and allowed to be slightly eccentric. You don't, after all, think of rooms with sets of four or six slipper chairs.

The original use of these little fireside chairs was intimate: The object was for the user to stay warm while getting dressed. Furthermore, one had to be in a position to pull on precious stockings without doing them any damage. To me the most noteworthy achievement of the upwardly mobile slipper chair is its progress from the boudoir and the dressing room to the library and the living room, not to mention the drawing room.

The nineteenth century, with its serious concern for comfort and its genius for new furniture types, turned the slipper chair into an engaging,

Especially low and tiny, the slipper chair above can be tucked in almost anywhere. The example below is surprisingly comfortable despite its diminutive size. Stanford White loved this chair and so do I.

decorative, and hugely useful piece. From the delicately framed seat for a lady's dressing room, it developed into a sturdy piece of upholstered furniture suitable for any intimate living-room conversation area. We are still talking about houses in which there was a rigorous distinction between informal living rooms and formal reception rooms furnished with stiff suites of furniture.

Gradually, of course, even the great drawing rooms succumbed to the appeal of informality. Rich, lush decoration is not necessarily precluded by an atmosphere of cozy intimacy. One of the major breakthroughs of interior decoration in the past 150 years is the domestication of grandeur. And by the Edwardian era, sitting rooms and drawing rooms were loaded with every conceivable sort of piece. Perhaps it was in reaction to this obvious excess that a stricter point of view prevailed for many years in this century. It is interesting to follow the history of slipper chairs as they move in and out of fashion.

At the turn of the century, the plump version that is still one of my favorites appeared in all sorts of rooms. In *The House in Good Taste* by Elsie de Wolfe (ghostwritten by Ruby Ross Wood) this chair can be seen in one illustration tucked between a sofa and a fireplace but also directly in the path of a door. Because of its diminutive scale, the chair does not completely block the way to the door. Nor does it conflict with any of the other furniture in the room. Stanford White used the same chair in the somber damask and silk velvet drawing room of the fabulous Mrs. Philip Lydig's town house, which was filled with sixteenth- and seventeenth-century paintings and furniture.

The shape of this wonderful little chair was later modernized by straightening the top line of the back, and it became a trademark of Billy Baldwin. Often Mr. Baldwin would design it with the simplest sort of tea-cozylike slipcover. Sometimes he would trim it with a band of braid around the bottom. The chair in one illustration, taken from an old *House & Garden* photograph of the beautiful living room in Hobe Sound that he did for the unbelievably chic Mrs. Clive Runnells of Lake Forest, has a white slipcover that has been trimmed with a navy-blue tape in a strict outline. A pair of these chairs sat in the middle of the room facing an arrangement consisting of a big sofa, two upholstered armchairs, and a coffee table. Larger chairs would have blocked the center of the room in a way that slipper chairs do not.

Another arrangement used both by Mr. Baldwin in his New York apartment on East 61st Street and by his mentor Mrs. Wood before him consisted of placing a pair of these chairs with their backs against a freestanding writing table on the side opposite the desk chair, simply waiting to be pulled into place wherever needed.

A model that has become popular in recent years is the tufted version with its gently curving back. The direct descendant of a very prevalent Victorian slipper chair, it has been simplified and refined and is often seen in the wonderfully romantic and inviting rooms of Mario Buatta. Sometimes it has a plain skirt with inverted corner pleats. Sometimes it has a shirred skirt or one that is box-pleated. It is equally at home covered in small printed materials and in large-scale chintzes. Patterns are not a problem with tufted furniture, although they seem to worry a lot of people. Actually, symmetrical patterns fit perfectly well into the orderly design of the tufting and asymmetrical patterns are no more difficult tufted than untufted.

The tufted slipper chair, I might add, need not be strictly identified with Victoriana. Like most upholstered furniture, it can blend perfectly well with contemporary or modern decoration simply by the elimination of all fussy details. It is easy to streamline the legs of practically any piece of upholstered furniture. And whereas the squared-off slipper chair seems to call for right angles, the more curved ones can sit happily when placed at any angle.

The Victorian chair above, with its curved and tufted back, has a seat large enough for any adult. It is also beautiful with turned legs showing. The sketch below shows Billy Baldwin's trim version of the chair directly across the page.

It is curious that the slipper chair was unknown in living rooms for long periods in decorating history, then popular in the nineteenth century, then unpopular for a fairly long time in this century. Now, and for the past several years, its popularity in living rooms is taken for granted. To be able to pull up a chair that is both comfortable and small is important in this day and age, when regimented conversation groups seem to be disliked. Its odd proportions are also a virtue: In a room full of sofas and chairs with similar back and seat heights, the monotony is pleasantly broken by the introduction of a chair or two that falls into a different category of scale. Chairs without arms are also easy to perch on, facing whichever side you want.

Most persuasive of all, perhaps, is the fact that you can use the versatile slipper chair where there is simply no room for another piece of furniture, and the most typical, practical, and traditional place is near a fireplace. There it sits, low enough not to look awkward, not blocking a favorite table covered with things you do not want to hide, contributing a great coziness. Doesn't everyone want to be beside the fire?

Like most pieces of furniture with a long history, the slipper chair is in vogue now for the same reasons that it was a hundred years ago. For form to follow function is not the purview of the twentieth century alone. Nothing in the realm of decorating is more vital than furniture that has evolved solely for the purposes of comfort and convenience.

BEDS AND BEDPOSTS

When my wife and I were looking for a pretty English bed for our Long Island bedroom, the Duchess of Marlborough, who keeps a small shop at Blenheim, found this one for us in partially polychromed mahogany. The bed curtains are a chintz called Tree Poppy, with a small-patterned lining. I had the top domed, which I find more pleasing than shirring stretched overhead. The bed is made up with old embroidered linens and a Marseilles coverlet. The small bookcase is Gothic Revival, a style I can't resist.

Do you remember the nice conservative bedrooms in the movies thirty or forty years ago? There were twin beds, usually in a sort of Colonial style. At the windows, there were Venetian blinds with organdy tie-back curtains and sometimes simple printed curtains over the tie-backs. The twin beds were pretty spartan, and when the mother and the father of the household—Spencer Tracy and Joan Bennett, for instance—went to bed, their robes were always laid neatly over the footboards. (If there was a crash in the driveway in the middle of the night, these robes would be put on and the belts tied before any investigation began.) During the day, the twin beds were covered with neat bedspreads made of chenille or some other plain material. This very chaste bedroom was obviously a carefully researched inter-pretation of the way nice people lived. People who weren't so nice had, in all honesty, better bedrooms. Take Scarlett O'Hara. Her Atlanta bedroom when she was the new Mrs. Butler was fabulous. In fact a lot of those gorgeous Hollywood ladies, when they were not playing role models, slept in bedrooms that looked outrageously sumptuous years ago and now look quite acceptably wonderful. The fact is that nondescript, boring bedrooms, far from being the right stuff, are simply disappointing and wrong-headed. As we all finally know, there is nothing the matter with a seductively sybaritic bedroom. It is no longer considered an error of taste. For many people, it never was.

Billy Baldwin always said that Sister Parish's ability to create luxurious feminine bedrooms was unequaled. No one could be more correct and well-bred than Mrs. Parish. Yet that has never stopped her from living in or creating for others bedrooms of great extravagance and luxury: spectacular curtains and valances with fringes and rosettes. . .beds hung with chintz or silk taffeta, the posts painted and carved and gilded. . .fat, puffy sofas with comfortable tea

where else can you get away with the untidy stacks of books that are so cozy looking in a bedroom?

tables or coffee tables in front of them. . . writing tables, chaise longues, gossamer throws to protect ankles from the cold (where on earth is the cold coming from, you might ask). . . pictures, objects, books, and memorabilia of all sorts everywhere. These are the things that give a bedroom the atmosphere that Billy so admired. They make it personal, and it is this element of the personal that leads to the intimacy that all really luxurious bedrooms have.

Your bedroom should be the most intimate and private room in the house. If it is not, then it is a little sad. The kind of personal indulgence I'm talking about shouldn't even be exposed to the criticism of others. It really *should* be private. A result of all this delicious privacy is the freedom to gather around yourself all the trappings of personal comfort and luxury. That does not necessarily mean gold boxes or Leonardo drawings. It means wonderful linens of whatever style or era you prefer, enough pillows and quilts and blankets to make you comfortable. If you hate beds covered with pillows, then by all means dispense with the pillows. The only dogma worth observing is one that is self-imposed. Extravagant flowers in your bedroom can be appreciated far more there than in another room. Some people, on the other hand, dislike sleeping in a room full of flowers. Again, preference, not rule, should govern.

There are collections that are too small or too silly or too arcane for more public rooms. They can be perfect in the bedroom. Sentimental objects and snapshots may look foolish in other rooms, yet in bedrooms they can be a source of great delight. Then there is the realm of personal utility: a writing table covered with charming implements and nicely engraved paper. . . beautiful files and boxes and folders to hold all the paper and writing materials. And finally, all the books. Where else can you get away with the untidy stacks of books that are delightfully cozy looking in a bedroom?

At last comes the centerpiece of this realm, the bed itself. Glamorous beds have always been fascinating, and they have certainly been plentiful in the history of furniture design. Canopy beds, more than any others, symbolize

rank and richesse, but they don't have to be pompous. They can be a lot of fun and have been for centuries. Tudor England produced carved and turned affairs that are solid, protective refuges from the outside world. Hung with some old velvet or crewel, these beds are practically rooms unto themselves.

In the seventeenth century, bed hangings became still richer than the Tudors' with astonishingly complicated patterns of galloon sewn on in curves and great, puckering scrolls. Spain and France and England all produced these tours de force of the artisan's skills. By the end of the seventeenth century,

Here is an American bed dressed up with a baldachin, which is a canopy style I sometimes use with upholstered headboards. The resident in this English cottage is the famous, now retired decorator Nancy Lancaster, a Virginian by birth.

My wife's dressing table in our New York bedroom is covered with white linen kept crisp and starched. On it stand silver picture frames, lacquer boxes, and crystal dressing table lamps from the twenties. The very old and worn Chippendale mirror above is a lovely contrast to the fresh linen.

upholsterers in England especially had developed their craft to such an elevated state that they were able to create beds of a breathtaking beauty and virtuosity that in my view have never been surpassed. Deeply carved Baroque canopy frames were entirely pasted with velvet or damask and then, glued into the seams, miles of frothy silk tassel fringe were used to complete the effect of staggering opulence. These prodigious canopies were sometimes suspended without posts from the ceiling and rose to heights of fifteen feet and more. They were divinely absurd.

In the eighteenth century, carved ornamentation became lighter in England and France as well as in the colonies. Lovely freestanding beds combined a fairly broad list of attributes—craftsmanship, practicality (those hangings did, after all, keep out the cold), luxury, self-expression, and beauty, not

Dressing tables are a marvelous element of bedroom decoration.

to mention comfort. French beds gained an even lighter appearance with the introduction of the smaller canopy supported by iron rods tapering inward from wooden posts, the rods then being swagged and tied with cords and tassels or elaborate rosettes. The bedrooms of Hubert de Givenchy's beautiful house near Chartres, often seen in photographs, are furnished with these graceful beds, called *lits à la polonaise*. M. Givenchy's rooms also exemplify another characteristic of many French bedrooms in that everything in the room—bed, curtains, and upholstery—is covered in the same patterned material, a device that gives a room great continuity and forms a superb background against which to arrange interesting furniture.

Unlike the grand state bed dominating a formal, albeit impersonal room, a dazzlingly luxurious bed can also be the focal point that permits a bedroom to contain many disparate aspects without looking disorderly. It can give to the room the scale that is required to subdue the presence of the books, the television (if there is one), and all the pictures and objects that might abound. If, on the other hand, you don't allow the clutter of books and TV sets, the great bed is just as pleasurable on its own. Its monumentality makes it exciting. Furthermore, adventures in drapery and upholstery are limitless. You don't even have to worry about experimenting; I can hardly imagine a design that hasn't already been tried in one way or another. Just remember that in most cases the bed should sit in the center of its wall.

One of the best twentieth-century adaptations of a previous style is the upholstered sleigh bed made popular by Syrie Maugham in the thirties. It is a design that still bears her name, and although interpretations vary from one upholsterer to another, the original proportions have survived more or less intact. The fact that so many successful adaptations have been made attests to the brilliance of Mrs. Maugham's idea. The bed in one black-and-white illustration is an example done with exuberant extravagance. The whole thing is covered in cream-colored satin and every edge is trimmed with a two-color tassel fringe. The idea of covering the entire surface of the frame of a piece of

All really luxurious bedrooms have a personal intimacy.

furniture with material was not new to Syrie Maugham, if we remember the English upholsterers of the seventeenth century. What Mrs. Maugham did was to apply their technique to a nineteenth-century piece, using a material that we all associate with the thirties. That's a pretty interesting combination. The rest of this room, which was decorated in 1936, conformed to the mood of the bed. The back-hanging was also cream satin. The floor was covered in white sheepskin, another of Mrs. Maugham's favorites. The walls and all the furniture were painted white. The bed was the focal point.

This marvelous bed design is often seen with tufting, a detail that works perfectly with the curves and the mood of a sleigh bed. A recent and very beautiful version was made by the firm of MAC II for Bill Blass and is covered in antique paisley, an idea that is both original and wonderfully decorative. Surrounding the bed, which comes out diagonally into the room from a corner, is a collection of paintings and drawings of enormous charm and beauty. The atmosphere of the room is one of pattern and mellow surfaces. Because of the exquisite pictures and the rarity of the antique paisley, there is also a mood of tremendous luxury. Nothing could be more different from the all-white environment of Mrs. Maugham's room. That, I suppose, is the test of a design. Just how many different ways can it be used? The answer, of course, is a good many indeed. And beds, if you stop to think about it, allow more room for fanciful design and the stamp of personal taste than any other single piece of furniture.

Dressing tables can be another marvelous element of decoration. My wife has a great knack with a simple table beautifully draped and skirted with old-fashioned linen and decorated with the traditional accoutrements. Is there anything prettier than the old mirrors and brushes and boxes and delicate lamps that appear on this appealingly feminine piece of furniture? A draped piece is also a perfect counterpoint to all the wood furniture that can so easily overwhelm the bedroom. Another antidote to wood is the odd piece or two of painted furniture.

Let me describe our bedroom, which through a no-color scheme is able to absorb a remarkable amount of furniture. The walls are hung with a pretty Chinese wallpaper which eliminates the need for any artwork—papered bedrooms are a classic kind of room anyway. The bed and windows are curtained in a silk that is the soft greenish gray of the background of the wallpaper. The French armoire is bleached and pickled. Two bookcases (not too tall) are painted the same off-white as the woodwork. There are three French chairs in old flaky paint, a Regency easy chair in its original gold leaf, and an antique chaise longue. All are covered in the same material as the curtains.

My wife's dressing table is skirted in Victorian embroidered white linen that echoes the antique linens on the bed. The bedside tables, once white lacquer, are now antiqued silver leaf. Over the dressing table hangs a Chippendale mirror in its original gilt. The little telephone table is silver and the low stool that holds books on my side of the bed is crumbling paint like the chairs.

The first impression of this room is the monochromatic tone: soft, silvery, and off-white. Except for the bright white linens, everything looks old and gently faded. Only later do you notice the amount of furniture—all of it very useful. The room is personal and marvelously comfortable, and that should be the goal of every bedroom.

Most upholsterers call this the Syrie Maugham bed after the designer who adapted an older sleigh bed design in the twenties. Mrs. Maugham trimmed this example with fringe in all the seams, as she often did, achieving an almost outrageous look of movie-star luxury heightened by her use of satin for the bed and the hangings behind it.

PARAMETERS OF FRAMING

Charles de Bestegui, art patron, and influential amateur decorator in the forties and fifties, designed his sitting room at the Plaza Hotel in New York in an almost Proustian English style. Prints and drawings in several kinds of frames are hung with careful symmetry on walls the color of a paper bag. The cool clear blue of the Victorian tufted pieces is a marvelous counterpoint to the deep green of the narrow-width carpeting and the curtains with their English swags and jabots.

One Saturday many years ago when I was an art-history student, I was an usher for a benefit tour of the Robert Lehman house on West 54th Street before the collection moved to the Metropolitan Museum. I was assigned to a room at the top of the house which was devoted to Mr. Lehman's collection of drawings by many artists from many periods and countries—Dürer, Leonardo, Rembrandt, and Fragonard, to name a few. The framing of the drawings reflected their individual types and dates. Two women who were among the throng of visitors that day moved silently from picture to picture. At the end one said to the other, "There's a fortune here in frames alone!" I wondered what she thought of Leonardo's drawing of a bear or of the pen-and-ink self-portrait by Dürer at age twenty-two. What was apparent, however, was their admiration of the framing. It seemed a pity to focus on the frames rather than the actual works of art within. Just as bad, though, is the practice of ignoring the importance of mats and frames or pretending that they do not really matter. They matter a lot and in a complex way because not only personal taste is involved. It is important to think about pictures and how they relate to one another and to the decoration of the rooms they hang in. And the frames are a part of all of this.

The architecture of the rooms in which pictures hang has historically carried great weight in the design of the frames used. One of my illustrations shows the original London setting of a life-size portrait by Sargent of the Marquess of Londonderry in the robes he wore to the coronation of Edward VII in August 1902. As one can see, the design of the vast frame relates exactly to the frames of the doorways that flank it. In the same way that the frescoed frames of painted ceiling and wall decoration of the sixteenth century integrated the artwork into the architectural scheme of the space, Lord Londonderry's

When I frame a number of pictures that are going to hang together, I use several framers to avoid a mass-produced look.

When this Sargent portrait hung in its original setting, shown here, the frame was part of the architecture of the room and the picture's impact was discreet. Today, minus the frame's pediment and minus the architecture, the Sargent dominates a New York apartment dining room.

gilt-wood frame allows the gigantic portrait to melt into the atmosphere of the room. Rather than hang on the wall, it becomes *part* of the wall. What is fascinating is that this marvelous Sargent now hangs in a New York apartment in the same frame you see here, minus its scrolled pediment. The original frame, in conjunction with its complementary architecture, had the effect of reducing the impact of the picture, whereas the present situation of the portrait has the opposite effect. The architecture is greatly reduced in scale, leaving no room for an enormous pediment, and the heroic size of the painting itself contributes greatly to a dazzling impression.

The most architectural treatment of picture framing I have ever seen, and one of the most successful, was executed by David Adler in the Lake Bluff, Illinois, house that he designed in 1926 for Mr. and Mrs. William McCormick

Blair. In the stair hall Mr. Adler, a man I admire more with every passing year, planned the panels of the pine walls to correspond to the size of a fine collection of Currier & Ives lithographs with the result that the paneling itself becomes the framing for the prints. It was a brilliant success, all the more so because it combined traditional, straightforward pine paneling with a tremendously original idea.

This is an example of a frame I had made for a set of prints in French mats. The frame's flat plane is painted a Pompeiian red and everything else is gilded except for the corner block medallions which are marbleized. The frame was finished by the decorative painter Paul Boyko.

No doubt the most common path to follow when selecting picture frames is that indicated by the period and country of origin of the work of art itself. The ebonized, deeply molded seventeenth-century Dutch frames with their minutely carved checkered patterns are perfectly suited to most paintings of that country and period. But they are also uncannily appropriate with big dark portraits of any era and with strong contemporary black-and-white drawings and prints; I can even imagine a dark Jasper Johns framed this way. Whether or not your decorating includes glass-and-chrome furniture or nineteenth-century plush dripping with fringe, these bold stylish frames are totally in keeping both with the forms of art mentioned and with the disparate styles of decoration individual collectors might favor.

Italian Renaissance frames possess the same infallible correctness with regard to paintings of their period and the task of blending in with different types of decoration. Here, however, one gets into a bit of a briar patch. The frames' architectural carving with pilasters and architraves and pediments is not conducive to reproduction and, to make matters worse, Renaissance frames often bear traces of faded polychromy. Copying this finish defies modern materials. So while fake Dutch frames are pretty easy to pull off, fake quattrocento ones are not. Now, if the latter is one cranked out by Duveen for J.P. Morgan in 1900, you might have a chance. Otherwise, you had better be careful and discreet.

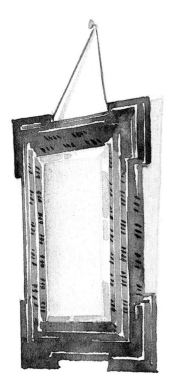

The ebony frame with stepped-out corners was made in many countries. Although the style reached a peak of popularity in the 17th century in Holland, a frame like this suits dark portraits of any era as well as contemporary black-and-white drawings. Such a frame is not hard to reproduce.

Care and discretion—the rule applies, I suppose, to all fakes or, rather, reproductions. Large-scale florid Spanish frames with their somewhat unrefined foliated scroll carvings and their bold juxtaposition of gold and black have an interestingly broad application to any framing lexicon, and they can be old or new. First of all, it will come as no surprise to hear that they look great on Spanish paintings. But it has been widely demonstrated in museums and galleries that they also look splendid on many contemporary pictures as well. Modern frames often lack the scale and the richness of material and surface that artworks seem to need in frames. There is something not very satisfying about polished steel and Plexiglas unless these two machine-age materials are closely related to the architecture or decoration of their surroundings. My feeling is that the crudeness of these Spanish frames corresponds with the insouciant energy of a great deal of twentieth-century painting.

Impressionist paintings are frequently framed in beautifully carved, gessoed, and gilded eighteenth-century French frames. In fact, Rococo frames are the conventional ones chosen for most Impressionist paintings. It is, of course, obvious that eighteenth-century French *anything* has an almost mystical ability to fit in, and the beauty of antique French frames is often on a par with the furniture in terms of the quality of the carving and the gilding. Fortunately for us all, these elaborate scroll- and flower-carved Louis XV frames and the simpler, more linear and architectural Louis XVI frames (in short, they resemble the furniture of their periods) have been made continuously for the past two hundred years, so there are a lot of old ones around. And if old ones are not within your reach, then remember the care-and-discretion rule and opt for the simplest interpretation possible and the *best*. Imitation gold leaf is worse than no gold at all.

There is a large and rather obscure category of picture frames which is of great interest. These are the frames designed by the artists themselves. At the loftiest extreme one could cite Jan van Eyck's illusionistic frames on which the artist has written an inscription or on the edge of which the portrait sitter rests his fingers. More recent examples include Seurat's Pointillist painted frames, Whistler's unmistakably chic frames composed of endless, finely reeded moldings (Whistler was almost *too* chic), and finally all those Aesthetic Movement painters who designed frames individually to relate to specific paintings. They are characteristic of a period of taste which was obsessed with ornament and decoration.

Our own period might also be called obsessive, and although it is seldom possible to commission grand frames for paintings of a significant scale, it is certainly possible to play around with the frames that one uses on prints and other works not weighed down with great importance or value. This, of course, requires a skillful and experienced framer. I have seen David Roberts prints of Egypt framed in bold Regency-style frames with an Egyptian flavor which in no way overwhelm the prints themselves and which play an important part in the decoration of the room. In recent years we have become accustomed to seeing botanical prints with brightly marbleized and generally painted-up frames and mats. It is interesting that this sort of extravagantly whimsical framing is OK with sets of prints. One alone doesn't seem to work. When I have to frame a number of prints and drawings and do not want them to have a mass-produced look, I divide them up among several framers. As a result, the finishing of the frames and mats varies. I also love scavenging around for old frames. Sooner or later you can find something to fit, and the beauty of old surfaces is always welcome. From time to time old mats are in acceptable shape and only require a new frame. Whether it is old or newly executed, a good French mat with its soft bands of watercolor wash and sepia outlines is one of the great ways to enhance an old print or watercolor. Double mats of contrasting board colors are another possibility.

The safety of works on paper is terribly important, and most good framers know enough about conservation principles that you don't have to worry. If you are unfamiliar with the shop's work, it is a good idea to be sure they use pure rag board for the mat and the proper kind of paste on the mount in order to avoid foxing and discoloration. There are also new types of glass that protect prints and drawings against fading in the light.

The subjective aspect of framing is very difficult to codify. In our time paintings have often been hung with no frames at all, and the result can be bold and stylish. Then there are the less successful experiments—for example, the uniform, skimpy frames on the works collected by The Museum of Modern Art in the early years, frames that defy the individuality of the paintings themselves. They also look cheap, and one of the essential qualities of art is that it is rare and special and oftentimes rich. If you must experiment, then put yourself in the hands of the best technician possible. In addition, you must study the history of framing, analyze your artwork and your taste, and finally make sure that you don't put up with a frame that is out of place in the decorative vocabulary of your house just because it happened to be on the picture when you bought it from the gallery. It would be crazily extravagant for a gallery to anticipate the taste of a picture's ultimate buyer, and so gallery frames are often cheap and ordinary. Frames, as I have said, are meant not only to set off pictures but also to relate them to the architecture and decoration of their surroundings—no element should be ordinary.

SETTING THE TABLE

Go set the table." Or, to be more polite, "Would you please help set the table?" The times I've heard this from the moment I could be trusted with breakable treasures! Do children still have to help set the table? I hope so. The endlessly repeated routine eventually results in being able to create the inviting personal arrangements that are central to attractive meals, and as we all know, everything happens at the dinner table.

The subject of table settings is broad and multifaceted. It embodies two opposite and very lively realms. The first is that of traditionalism; the second is that of fashion and change—two areas of concern that can be antithetical to many people. But the combination of these opposing themes—old-fashioned on the one hand and up-to-date on the other—is what leads to the delightful tables that make some households memorable and that finally confer laurel crowns on those really legendary hostesses (and hosts).

Without sounding too partial to the illustrious history of the magazines of the Condé Nast company, I must say that while growing up, I was continually entertained by their frequent articles about various personalities and their tables for lunch and dinner, breakfast and tea, as well as every other conceivable repast. There was Valentina's round table with its centerpiece, a monumental 1860s Baccarat candelabra that looked like something from *La Traviata*. Massed around its base were scarlet and burgundy carnations (everyone hates carnations now, but they looked awfully good then) combined with cherries, lemons, and limes, on an embroidered white cloth with hammered-copper service plates on which sat blue-and-white Chinese rice bowls for soup with matching porcelain spoons at each place. The silver was large-scale and simple, as was the crystal. More disparate elements could not be imagined. The result was beautiful.

Then there was Harvey Ladew, the Baltimore patrician whose house and garden were famous for their style. He served breakfast to his guests on trays bearing porcelain decorated with hunting motifs, a silver bell made in the shape of a fox's head, and silver flatware with rough horn handles. When she wasn't thinking about her newest bangle from Cartier, the Duchess of Windsor, another Baltimorean, dreamed up silver with real bamboo handles—or copied it as soon as she saw it. The table at the Windsors' mill outside Paris photographed in the early fifties was full of charming ideas that are just as appealing today. In addition to the bamboo-handle silverware, there were painted faience plates, overscaled crystal, and a basket in the center shaped like a cornucopia and filled with primroses.

My favorite magazine table setting was the long Georgian pedestal table of the legendary Elsie Woodward with its vast collection of eighteenth-century Waterford glass. The centerpiece of this divine table was a crystal temple with a pagoda-shaped roof and a mirrored base. It was this lovely object, rare and glamourous, that prevented the table from looking stuffy and conventional. Furthermore, and here is where the contemporary fashion element comes in, the place mats were made of plastic decorated with gold Art Moderne scrolls. Heaven knows I hate plastic anything, and plastic place mats sound awful today. But who cares! In the forties they were undoubtedly diverting. That table has to have been gorgeous.

Starting with the first thing to be put on the table, linens are an easy and beautiful way to change your look, especially if you do not have many sets of dishes to play around with and if you are or have someone who can do a lovely job of ironing. In the past fifteen or twenty years there has been a revolution in the design of table linens, especially attractive and interesting napkins that can be used with plain mats or tablecloths. There are informal batiks and ginghams and plaids and an equally large range of more formal types with appliqué or embroidery. Old ones are nicer to the touch because they have become pleasantly soft with years of laundering. Napkins with synthetic fibers feel stiff and awful. The pleasure we all anticipate when we sit down to eat is not one that admits thoughts of polyester.

Place mats can be just as beautiful as tablecloths, and if your table has a wonderful top, the mats can be just large enough for the dinner plate to sit on. Round tables do not look very good with oblong place mats overlapping or bumping into one another at odd angles. Years ago I saw a marvelous table set with old cross-stitched place mats and napkins, antique pink lusterware plates, and amethyst glass. Down the center of the table were tiny bunches of pink and lavender flowers also in amethyst glass. It was charming and American and

informal but still very chic. It was also wonderfully personal in the way it showed a collection in use instead of on display.

If you have the space to store it, glassware and porcelain can be collected throughout your life and will enable you to satisfy both the need to collect and the desire to have variety in your table settings. A range of components can enable you to experiment with all kinds of different looks: napkins folded in fanciful ways, plates and soup bowls mixed in unexpected combinations, and the general realm of glass and crystal clustered together one way one time, another way another time. (How many people do we know whose tables always look the same!) Obviously, collecting different patterns of silverware is beyond the reach of most of us, but if you can afford it, that's certainly fun.

The various accessories that can be put on the table don't necessarily have to match. There are a great many objects that can give a table an invitingly cluttered look if that's what you like. Saltcellars, pepper shakers or pepper mills, mustard pots, antique boxes for toothpicks or artificial sweeteners, little pitchers and sauceboats, jam pots—these old-fashioned minutiae can lend a generous atmosphere to a table which conveys a sense of anticipating the guests' individual needs. Customs change, of course, and we live in a time when smoking at the table is suddenly scorned. Eighty years ago, no one would have dreamed of smoking at the table, and if a hostess today wants to return to that point of view, why make a fuss? If there are any smoking accessories on the table, then one may smoke. If they are absent, one should take the hint.

The centerpiece of this chapter should probably be the centerpiece of the table. It should be the best part, except for the food, of course, or the conversation. Here's where the cheerful homemaker can really make a difference. New ideas are always welcome. Ages ago Bernard Boutet de Monvel, the great portrait painter, combined real vegetables with a collection of old faience

Here is a centerpiece lesson from Bernard Boutet de Monvel, the society portrait painter, who devised this table decoration in the forties for his mill outside Paris. On compotes from the dessert service he combined faience vegetables with real fruit— a wonderful way to enliven porcelain objects.

> The centerpiece should be the best part, except for the food or the conversation, of course.

In her Georgian dining room with its Coromandel screen in the background, Mrs. William Woodward loaded her dining table with objects of crystal and glass, building on the impact of the rare and glorious crystal pagoda in the center.

ones to create a wonderful arrangement that could be copied today. Old tureens and their smaller matching covered dishes clustered in the middle of the table can be lovely and sufficiently low to make the view across the table unobstructed. The modern practice of numerous tiny vases filled with a variety of small flowers can be pretty, fairly easy, and quick. (You have to have a florist who has something other than 'American Beauty' roses and daisies, though.) Antique glass and porcelain dishes piled with fruit look lovely and do not run the risks that arranging flowers in water always poses. Flower arranging, the most time-honored method of creating a centerpiece, is always best, I think, where some personal touch has been developed. The most personal touch of all is to have grown the flowers oneself. Is there anything more enchanting than a bunch of homegrown roses glowing in the candlelight? Even if you have to rely on your florist, you can learn to take at least a little control of the situation. Most bought centerpieces are too tall and stiff, but all they need is a stern hand and a little self-confidence.

Finally, if it's dinnertime, the possibilities that candles provide is enormous. Antique candlesticks of all sorts can be mixed with silver in a carefree way as long as they look pretty. Low candles, tall candles, votive candles—they are all beautiful. Color is important. I love cream-colored and ivory-colored candles, and white ones naturally. I also love black candles, which look marvelous but which some people find creepy. What I don't like are colored candles, unless it's Christmas. And certainly candles should not have a scent that competes with the food.

The most gratifying aspect of collecting all the various things that are required for setting the table is the way in which one can mix purchases and presents and inherited bits and pieces from the eras of one's life in such a way that the table, when all dressed up for dinner, looks beautiful, inviting, and personal. After more than two decades of picking up some soup bowls here and some dessert plates there, my wife and I still use many of the things we started out with: strict early Georgian-style silver with heavy pistol-handle knives, which looks older than it is because we use it every day; plates decorated with fruit and flowers, which are preceded by red-and-gold Wedgwood service plates that belonged to my wife's grandmother and which are now often combined with a collection of nineteenth-century ruby glass tumblers and vases that have increased in number with the passing years. (I should mention that the walls of the dining room are glazed in two reds.)

Our candlesticks are either glass or silver, depending on the number required, and the small objects such as saltcellars and ashtrays match the candle holders. If you have vermeil candlesticks, I don't mean to say you have to use them with vermeil knives and forks; too much matching looks store-bought. The wine coasters we use are either red lacquer, emphasizing the red motif, or silver. Sometimes we put the wine into old decanters; other times we leave it in the bottle.

As we get older, we seem to grow fonder of heavily embroidered tablecloths. Our napkins don't change much—they are all big, white, linen, damask, and from another era. Every year a few more of them go to shreds, but that's no real problem since they were always made in such huge sets.

The flowers in the center are arranged in any number of interesting vases in a variety of sizes. Some of them are antique red glass; others are old Baccarat or Waterford glass or pressed glass from the nineteenth century. Their intrinsic value is beside the point. What makes them desirable is their capacity to hold flowers in an easy and attractive way. It seems best to choose flowers that are not excessively fragrant—we avoid narcissus and lilies—but not many flowers can dominate the aroma of hot food.

The dessert things we use are sometimes pink with flowers in the center or old green Wedgwood majolica. The real point is that there are no restrictions on what you can collect and combine just as long as you are fairly sure of what you like. It is the ability to change from one day to the next that enlivens table setting. Maybe we shouldn't ask the kids to set the table after all. Grownup creativity is more reliable than a child's improvisations.

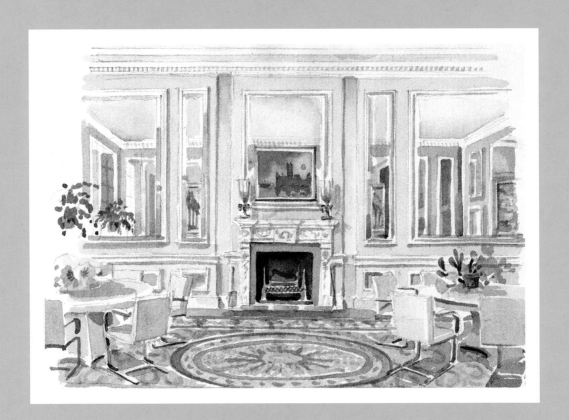

PATTERN UNDERFOOT

A large and splendid sixty-year-old rug by Pontremoli in petit point and needlepoint, found in London, supplies most of the color and pattern in Anne Bass's New York dining room, which I recently decorated. Into the paneling I set beveled mirror glass on all sides of the room to add light and a sense of illusion. There are two identical painted Empire-style tables with Mies chairs. Over the 18th-century English fireplace hangs Monet's view of the Houses of Parliament and the Thames.

I can't imagine what got into everybody, allowing plain floors and plain carpets to take over the way they did years ago. It was probably the dreadful combination of inflation and the lack of craftsmanship, that sad state that hangs over us like a cloud and has ruined a lot of delightful building practices in this era of mass production. In recent years, however, the battle for rich design in flooring has gained considerable ground; Modernists and traditionalists alike have rediscovered the infinite possibilities that lie underfoot.

Patterned floors exist historically and geographically in a huge variety of materials and designs. Mosaic paving, said to have originated in Greece, was made throughout the Roman Empire. From England to Africa, Romans produced mosaic floors of marvelous quality and legendary durability. The surface of these floors was a little rough, made of tiny marble tesserae and sometimes bits of glass, tile, and even chalk.

With its Greco-Roman heritage and its early tradition of design vitality, Italy played an important role in style throughout Europe for centuries. Elaborately patterned marble floors made of large, smooth pieces of varying colors exist everywhere in Italy and can be remarkably similar in buildings that are remarkably dissimilar. They survive from every period. The most elaborate designs were obvious tours de force of skillful labor as well as design brilliance. The extraordinary intricacy of the patterns, however, often belie the economical use of the material involved. By incorporating relatively small pieces of marble in the design there was a minimum of waste.

An interesting example of the development of floor patterns from mosaic to larger patterns can be seen in and around Venice. In San Marco there are panels of designs made up of tiny pieces of black, white, and terra-

This is a parquet floor in a crisp contemporary pattern that I designed seventeen years ago. The oak boards are alternately stained a honey color and bleached ivory white. The floor was made by Bill Erbe.

A good floor says that the entire foundation of the room is sound.

cotta-colored marble. The same patterns and the same marbles are to be seen in gradually increasing scale in numberless later churches in the area. By the sixteenth century this tricolored paving becomes so enlarged that the design of a small panel of mosaic at San Marco can fill the entire bay between each pair of pilasters in, for instance, San Giustina in nearby Padua.

A floor that exists everywhere—England, France, Germany—is, of course, the floor of squares of light stone with a diamond of dark marble at the corners where the lines intersect. I always suspected that this pleasant design was a solution to the problem of chipping corners.

In houses and palaces, grand patterned marble floors were more or less confined to halls and spaces of great formality. Carpets were (and are) the most common way of achieving pattern underfoot. We are all accustomed to decorating with Oriental carpets of every kind. European factories have lent their names to entire carpet types—Axminster, Savonnerie, and Aubusson—which remind us of the skill and taste of the eighteenth century. Needlepoint and Bessarabian rugs, very much in fashion now, were never really out. And in the past twenty-five years, beginning especially with the carpet designs of David Hicks, patterned carpet by the yard has once again, as in so much of the nineteenth century, become indispensable in the field of interior decorating.

The desire for pattern on the floor has also inspired all kinds of experiments with paint. For centuries architects and decorators have painted and stenciled simple wooden floors to resemble more elaborate parquet or marble. Even carpet designs painted in trompe l'oeil crop up now and then, some naïve and modest, others, like those created by Renzo Mongiardino, skillful fantasies of whimsical extravagance for very rich people in search of something new.

Then, of course, there is the whole familiar terrain of tiles: terra-cotta tiles from Italy and Spain and Mexico, Minton's tiles from England, and French tiles, which, characteristically, cover the entire spectrum of tile design and manufacture.

Rarer, more durable than carpet and certainly more precious, are patterned parquet floors. There are two philosophies in the design of parquet floors. One is to treat the wood as though it were marble. Typically Italian parquet floors can be so intricate that it is difficult to imagine making them out of wood. Russian palaces, often designed by Italians after all, have numerous equally elaborate parquet floors.

In France and Germany, the philosophy governing the design evolution of parquet floors appears to have taken into account a little more seriously the actual properties of a wooden board. Laid out at right angles to the walls or on the diagonal, these more geometric floors were less spectacular than the Italians' but they performed a more coherent role in blending architecture and decoration: ornamental enough to adorn carpetless spaces, simple enough in design and manufacture to be used in great suites of adjoining rooms, some of which were to have carpets. The early eighteenth-century Charlottenburg Palace in Berlin has wonderful floors made of squares composed of triangles that are separated by long lines of planks, some running diagonally and some running at right angles. The result is a simple design that viewed from different angles can appear to be squares or diamonds or even hexagons, yet the effect is not nervous making.

The most famous and enduring parquet design of all is the one known as parquet de Versailles. From the seventeenth century until the present day, this wonderful oak flooring has been used continuously in buildings of every type. I hate to tell you that it is even made in vinyl, but let's just try to forget that. It was originally made up of oak pieces held together by their tongue-and-groove edges and by mortise and tenon (these days glue). Then as now, it was manufactured in panels and then assembled in the room. Because of this practice, parquet de Versailles has always lent itself to being dismantled and preserved. Bill Erbe, the grandson of the founder of the William J. Erbe company, America's greatest provider of fine wooden flooring, can still take you through storerooms where squares of parquet de Versailles stand on edge in bins. Mr. Erbe can also make new parquet as can several other floor makers who are lucky enough to have preserved the necessary skills.

The amazing thing about parquet de Versailles is that it has been a highly desirable and appropriate floor in Baroque, Rococo, Neoclassical, and even contemporary interiors. That is a very good track record. The design consists basically of meter-square panels, set on the diagonal and separated and framed by bands of two or three boards. Inside the squares is a pattern composed of short strips and squares of wood that are arranged in an interlocking design rather like basket weaving.

France is full of this terrific flooring and thank goodness, because for the last hundred years we have been cheerfully cannibalizing French houses in renovation or demolition with the happy result that American houses and apartments sport a fair amount of the real thing. Imagine how marvelous it is nowadays to be able to lay down antique parquet. Because it is completely handmade and hand sanded, it has an undulating surface that gives it a soft appearance unique to all very old things. New parquet in the Versailles pattern is very beautiful, too. However much one loves it, though, it cannot compare with period flooring.

English houses, not known for extravagant parquet, occasionally have parquet de Versailles floors. Boughton, built early in the eighteenth century and hugely influenced by French architecture of the time, has floors exactly like those of Versailles. Eighteenth-century American houses rarely have patterned parquet floors. A wonderful exception is Monticello. I think it is typical of the genius of Thomas Jefferson that he would insist on having beautiful, atypical floors.

It can come as no surprise to hear that in the nineteenth century parquet floors became so complicated that they often ceased to look like floors at all. At Fountainebleu there are nineteenth-century floors by Poncet made up of fifteen different kinds of wood. The pattern is as complicated as that of a marquetry commode. Another trick of Victorian floor designers was to leave the center field as plain as they thought was possible, that is, basket weave or herringbone. Over this a carpet would be laid, and they would fill the border with patterns of fretwork or interlocking Greek key designs made of several kinds of wood.

There is a kind of basic quality achieved by a good floor. It seems to say that the entire foundation of the room is sound and good. In an era of dry-wall construction and clip-on window mullions, it is easy to understand why something as fundamental as a handsome parquet floor gives to a room such a feeling of real structural integrity and luxury. The very fact that we *walk* on floors makes them all the more welcoming when they are fine.

I can't imagine what got into everybody years ago, allowing plain floors and carpets to take over.

One of the best rooms in New York is an entrance hall designed for William Paley by Jansen in the early sixties. The floor is the key element in the room, both architecturally and decoratively. It is Italian, probably late eighteenth century or early nineteenth. The designs are strongly geometric and the woods are walnut, maple, and cherry. The entire space is organized by the bold scale of the parquet, the patina of which is responsible for the great character of the room.

If I were restoring an old house with good parquet floors, I would make any sacrifice to preserve them. If I were building a new house, I would, similarly, make any sacrifice in order to be able to include some marvelous parquet, whether old or new. Nothing could give more lasting pleasure or survive more changes in decorative style.

For Mr. and Mrs. Deane Johnson's front hall in Southampton we had a thin velvet-weave carpet made in Paris which is based on an early 19th-century design of flower wreaths. The table is Gothic Revival; beside it stands a Victorian hall chair.

styles

VICTORIAN COMEBACK

When Michael Taylor decorated this room in a California Victorian house, he had authentic proportions, period plasterwork, and the original fireplace to work with. He furnished the room in a Victorian mode but took many liberties which make the room surprising and light instead of serious and museumlike. For example, the wallpaper is Victorian in its strong patterning but is actually Chinese; the furniture is twice removed from the real thing, being Taylor's interpretation of Syrie Maugham's interpretation of what the Victorians did.

How many years has it been since you last heard the gloomy prediction that pretty soon even Victorian furniture would be back in style? You might have heard it ten or fifteen years ago, but you sure don't hear it any more. Victorian is definitely back. Why the vogue for this style of decoration is so widespread now is difficult to explain. There is a mania for new fashion that keeps decorating addicts churned up and imitating each other year in and year out, but why Victorian? Perhaps, as in the nineteenth century, it is the general prosperity that enables people to turn their attention to a style of decorating symbolic of financial ease; Puritanism isn't exactly a driving force in the world of the happy consumer nowadays. But simple momentum is surely a major cause. Don't for a minute think that a bunch of fashion coordinators sat down a few years ago and mapped out a strategy aimed at promoting a rebirth of the Victorian style. There have always been individuals with a special love for decorating in the various nineteenth-century modes. While some trends of the past twenty years have come and gone, decorating in the Victorian taste has been practiced all along with great skill by an increasing variety of people. Their influence, regardless of other forces, has been of prime importance.

The decorator whose way with things Victorian first entered my consciousness was Madeleine Castaing, who in spite of her great age operated a shop of incredible charm on the Left Bank in Paris. Mme. Castaing's rooms were published constantly in the years after the Second World War. She revived a great number of mid-nineteenth-century designs, and with them she created a decorating vocabulary that was very personal and hugely influential in the work of others. There were chairs and stools with frames of wood carved in the form of twisted rope; there were carpets densely patterned with leaves

The Deane Johnson's mid-19th-century house in Southampton has a red-walled living room with a Brussels tapestry carpet from Paris on the floor. We collected Victorian furniture—mostly English—with an eye toward comfort and eccentric shape. Festoon blinds and lace shades hang at all the windows.

and palm fronds and flowers, usually on very dark grounds; there were numberless little tufted chairs and settees in fantastic shapes; and everything was lit by lamps with tiny peaked lampshades lacquered Bristol blue or brilliant green. Her patterned materials resembled the shawls worn by the women in Ingres portraits. Brass canopy beds were draped with miles of starchy dotted swiss. Bookcases and desks were often Regency or Biedermeier. Gothic motifs were a great favorite. These wonderful rooms were funny-looking in the best possible way. There was a distinct unwillingness to be too serious. What counted was a rather hilarious prettiness, obvious comfort, and a bit of the desire to surprise. It was a rarefied taste, but it was very chic, and it certainly did spread. Billy Baldwin, with his genius for fashion, created a number of rooms using carpets and patterned materials that were among the Castaing staples. Diana Vreeland's red sitting room on Park Avenue was the most famous of these dense, moody rooms. If tasseled and fringed décor wasn't exactly the rage in the fifties, there were enough people marching to that distant drum to keep the beat alive.

Some twenty years ago, Albert Hadley took me to see the New York apartment of Mr. and Mrs. Joshua Logan, where he was working at the time. I cannot remember what I expected to see, but it certainly was not the marvelous fantasy that greeted my eyes. The vast drawing room overlooking the East River had dark walls glazed a warm, deep red. The floor was covered with an enormous quantity of antique Brussels tapestry carpet. Strewn—and I mean strewn—across the flowered carpet was a collection of I suppose French and English chairs. The frames of these wonderful chairs were made in various fanciful shapes, and their covers were a combination of velvet and tapestry, twisted and shirred and corded in ways appropriate to their original designs. Nothing had been simplified. No details had been omitted. Fringes of extravagant complication finished everything off. The atmosphere was intensely warm and comfortable. I felt like Aladdin entering the cave. I was seeing what I felt was the best possible interpretation of a then rare and offbeat style, an example of truly personal taste. (Can there be any goal more sought-after in decorating than that of expressing personality and individuality?) Furthermore, all of this atmosphere was achieved through decoration. The architecture of the building was not Victorian. One of the most compelling aspects of the Victorian style is the fact that it has often been achieved by decorative and not by the architectural means, a fact that contributes greatly to its applicability today.

At the same time that the Logans were collecting and decorating in their way, Betty Sherrill of McMillen was using Victorian furniture in her way to furnish her graceful house in Southampton. The Sherrills' house, far from being anonymous architecturally, is a rambling Shingle Style example of that uniquely American phenomenon, the summer cottage. Built in the last years of the nineteenth century for Elihu Root, it is a deliciously complicated house that was once, no doubt, full of dark wood and heavy drapery. Now it is light and airy. The color schemes are typical of those perfected by the firm of McMillen: pale greens and yellows and a dozen shades of white, that most complicated of colors. To punctuate this pastel palette, Mrs. Sherrill used a quantity of Victorian furniture in its original black paint decorated with flowers and mother-of-pearl inlay. The effect was—and is—one of charming playfulness and coziness.

Also in Southampton and just a stone's throw away is a house decorated by Billy Baldwin in the fifties. The house itself is huge and ponderous. Everything has been painted white, from the heavy architectural woodwork to the tables and chairs that are probably from the 1850s. Leggy and curvy, it is the sort of furniture you expect to find in Natchez, Mississippi. But painted white, it relinquishes all its fussiness and none of its charm. The upholstery is

This Italianate Victorian house in red brick and limestone is in Greencastle, Indiana, and I have known and loved it all my life. It has turrets and towers, quoins, brackets, balconies, and architectural references of all kinds. It was built in the middle of the 19th century and is such an American type that you could see this exact same house in California or in Maine.

dont for a minute think that a bunch of fashion coordinators sat down and mapped out the rebirth of the Victorian style.

the beautiful tulip pattern from Margaret Owen, that marvelous and now-lamented fabric house.

These three rooms were all done twenty or thirty years ago, and incredibly they seem more in fashion now than when they were first seen: comfortable and amusing and not too serious. Rigid styles are limiting in every way, but the world of Victoriana is very permissive. Its impurity is its virtue.

In 1964, Mario Praz published a book entitled *An Illustrated History of Furnishing.* It is a book noteworthy, among other things, for its illustrations, which consist largely of minutely executed and unbelievably lovely watercolors of nineteenth-century interiors from throughout Europe. Every decorator knows this book and it has been an inspiration to many.

The rooms influenced by Praz (as well as the Logans' apartment) were more European than American. Surfaces and materials were rich and very complicated. As in the days of Queen Victoria, every period from the past was utilized: Turkish carpets, Renaissance bronzes, seventeenth-century delft-ware, sixteenth-century majolica, Chinese porcelains, plus a copious supply of Victorian copies and interpretations of every conceivable period. These rooms in the European Victorian style that began to appear with greater and greater frequency were noteworthy for their deeply comfortable atmosphere and whimsical richness. Now that the style is firmly fixed in our line of vision, we are accustomed to it. Not so many years ago it was very unfamiliar. However, there were several practitioners already established in the genre seen in Praz.

In New York, the firm of Denning & Fourcade has for almost thirty years been creating rooms that appear to be waiting for the reincarnation of Princesse Mathilde. While glass and chrome furniture was getting scratched and chipped all over America, Robert Denning and Vincent Fourcade were busily re-creating an atmosphere of shadowy luxury that made you forget the world outside. And that, of course, was the point. In the midst of the Industrial Revolution, when Europe was torn up by the construction of new railways and streets and factories, it must have been wonderfully comforting to come home to your Renaissance Revival town house or your Louis Quatorze-style apartment. And sure enough, after a couple of hours of gridlock, it is heaven today to stoop under a Genoese velvet portiere and set foot on a dusky Persian-made

Ziegler carpet (When asked about plain carpet, Bob Denning replied with a laugh that he "couldn't conceive of using it") as you head for some piece of enveloping Victorian furniture made for the well-fed entrepreneurs of the 1870s. Moreover, if you have any interest in arts and crafts there is something very encouraging in the late 1980s to see what wondrous handwork can still be done.

The people who love the actual work of decorating also love working with the craftsmen who produce it. As the fashion for Victorian decoration gains in popularity, the number of people who can execute the necessary finishes increases. It's the old law of supply and demand, and it's a very happy situation. Europe is still the training ground of these craftsmen. No discussion of this type of work would make any sense without mentioning two seminal forces in what my stereo man calls the state of the art. Renzo Mongiardino and the late Geoffrey Bennison have created a continuous stream of work in the past few decades that has brought with it a band of workmen who can stencil and marbleize and create faux anything with remarkable skill and charm. Old lace and velvet is skillfully mended and patched and reused in rooms where all traces of the present seem to melt away. The advent of this sort of work seems to me to be almost a public service, insuring for the future a steady supply of the sort of workmanship that cheers anyone who blanches when home computers are mentioned.

The room in the watercolor is to me a perfect example of the amazing combinations that come together to create a popular style. It is a room done a few years ago in California by the late Michael Taylor, another decorator whose ability to translate and interpret fashion went on for many years. The house itself is Victorian and retains its plasterwork and its fireplace. The upholstered furniture is derived from Victorian models, but, and this is what I find so amusing, it is also derived from the great Syrie Maugham, a decorator about whom Michael Taylor knew a great deal. She was simply playing around with Victorian furniture, to which she gave a new look. Michael Taylor's interpretation moves closer to the original style, but the colors are of our time and the fringes and tassels look light and fluffy rather than heavy. The walls are very patterned in a way appropriate to a nineteenth-century paper. Actually it is a Chinese paper that we more often associate with Rococo rooms. But the effect is just right: amusing, colorful, and unpredictable. There is no question about the beauty or the comfort of this room. There is also no question about whether or not it is in style. Pin any date on it: It embodies the appeal of decoration that is at present in fashion and will never, thank goodness, be seriously out of fashion.

CLASSICISM IS ALWAYS NEW

Chiswick House, Lord Burlington's personal casino for parties on the outskirts of London, was designed by his lordship, a talented amateur Palladianist, and his even more talented protégé, William Kent. This masterful circa-1725 villa was based on the Villa Rotonda built by Palladio outside Vicenza around 1550. Both buildings have been monumentally influential. Kent's virtuoso interiors include an octagonal hall and a circular chamber. His doorways and friezes, chimney-pieces and ceilings reflect the grandeur of his patron's bold conception.

Decoration, like architecture, has been enlivened with great regularity by revivals of a classicizing nature. To deal with all of them, in fact even to list all of them, is well beyond the scope of these paragraphs. But several of them have influenced subsequent generations of architects and designers and have actually changed the way we see things. These revivals are worth reviewing.

Palladio is a household word. He must be the most famous architect in history. In the sixteenth century he designed a number of buildings inspired by ancient Rome that to this day are a source of inspiration to architects and designers everywhere. It is always fascinating to contemplate the achievement of Palladio and the gigantic effect he has had over the past four hundred years. The beauty of his buildings is easy to perceive. Less easy for us to weigh are his dazzling originality and boldness and the impact these qualities had on his contemporaries, an impact that was enormous. He was, for instance, the first architect to take what looks like the portico of a Roman temple and put it on the front of a house. This device alone has supplied architects with a seemingly inexhaustible source of ideas ever since.

Less than one hundred years later (it is easy to forget how close in time they were), Inigo Jones applied some of his new knowledge about Palladio to buildings and additions to buildings in seventeenth-century England. A century after that, a community of architects and decorators turned their passion for Palladio into a strict school of architecture and thus began a hundred years of a style we know as Georgian. I cannot think of anything as long-lasting as that movement. By the middle of the eighteenth century, Pompeii and Herculaneum had been exposed to view, and another electrifying wave of Classicism was charging through drafting rooms and drawing rooms.

What made this new Classical Revival so vigorous was not its ability to draw on detailed archaeological references. It was the originality and the brilliant reapplication of the new material that inspired professionals and their clients forever after. Robert Adam, its star, lent his name to a style just as Palladio had done. In addition to Adam and his family, there were endless architects who worked in the same mode. Originality was not at an end either. Sir John Soane's unique vision resulted in a body of work that, like Palladio's, drew on sources similar to those of his contemporaries but that were amazingly original and that helped pave the way for still another classical mania—the Greek Revival. By the 1840s, every farming town in America, not to mention major cities, had a bank or a house or a church that was a tiny replica of the Parthenon. Like the Palladian wave before it, the Greek Revival movement has remained a continuous presence in the world around us.

Starting in the eighteenth century, revival architects left us with an extra heritage, one that has a practical as well as decorative use. They designed and made furniture. I might add that some of them designed almost anything they could get their hands on, from watch fobs to carriages. Classical revival furniture designed by architects, especially when it was designed for a particular spot in a specific room, takes on an interest that furniture intended for production in quantity often lacks. Not that the designs in the famous cabinetmakers manuals are boring; there is a difference, however, in concept, and the marvelous thing about a lot of this architect-designed furniture is that it has a boldness of scale and ornamentation that places it in a decorative category all its own. Although it was designed to be seen *en suite* with closely related architectural details, this big, assertive furniture is, paradoxically, often perfect in twentieth-century rooms, especially rooms that lack architectural detail. The tables, cabinets, pedestals, and urns that began to appear in the 1720s are so packed with architectural references that they can help fill the characterless spaces that are such a problem in newly built apartments and houses.

Palladian houses of the sixteenth century were, of course, filled with Renaissance furniture. When the Georgian followers of Palladio were faced with the problem of furnishing their houses, they turned to Italianate motifs for inspiration, and the result was often original to the point of bizarreness. And it was almost always wonderfully rich and complicated. William Kent (1685–1748) was a "painter, architect, and the father of modern gardening," in Horace Walpole's words. The furniture he designed as well as the furniture he inspired has a lush quality that gives any room an atmosphere of luxury. It is also often rather eccentric to our eyes. His gigantic console tables are composed of scrolls and swags and masks and shells and even complete figures carved in the round, sitting on the stretchers not in order to support the tops but apparently just to strike a pose. Surfaces are covered with superb carving. His chairs and settees, rarer than his tables, have great foliate motifs that wrap around the legs and backs and sometimes simply become the legs.

The more conservative Kent-style furniture—mahogany rather than painted or gilded pine, and smaller in scale—consists of a wealth of secretaries and bookcases that have, as their chief ornamentation, pediments and columns and pilasters. Occasionally, a cabinet may be a scaled-down version of an almost complete building, starting with a rusticated base, and ending with a pedimented attic story resting on a complete entablature with minutely carved columns. The great appeal of this furniture lies not only in its overall beauty but in its perfect scaling, especially in the small pieces. A small secretary is short as well as narrow and the details in a so-called dwarf piece are as minute as the object itself.

Robert Adam (1728–92) was the son of a Scottish architect. He was clearly a genius in the realm of drawing and designing. In the 1750s he went to Rome. For the next three years, he traveled and studied and made copious notebooks of drawings. His book on Diocletian's palace in Spalato (Split), in what is now Yugoslavia, was the result of this tour. So was the inspiration for the rest of his life's work. From the time he returned to England and set up his architectural practice in London in 1758 until his death thirty-four years later, he created designs for furniture in a Neoclassical style that have continued to inspire furniture makers with few interruptions ever since.

The reach of Adam's architectural conceptions is remarkable. A house designed by him gives, from the moment your foot touches the step and your hand grasps the iron railing, the impression of a complete integration of decoration and architecture. The balusters of the railing you hold, the lanterns overhead, the doorknob and the carving around the door are all composed from the same design lexicon used for the architecture itself. Once inside, you

In Lincoln Kirstein's New York brownstone there is a space that is both drawing room and art gallery, and this room received a Neoclassical treatment. I draped the walls with pale gold cotton moiré with so-called stone valances that resemble carving and placed columns on the end walls. The furniture is Beidermeier, a Neoclassical style of central Europe around 1830.

Using overscale furniture and decoration is not treacherous; it just requires a little advance planning.

find that this application of design motifs continues in an all-pervasive way. I do not mean to imply that I find it monotonous, although some do, of course. That, however, is not the point. The effect that Adam had on furniture design is what interests us and what is responsible for the world's great supply of Adam-style furniture.

Try, if you can, to forget the connotations that the words "Adam Style" usually bring to mind—the dinky plaster-of-Paris medallions and swags pasted on mantels, or Wedgwood-type plaques incorporated into sconces. All these things with their plastic doodads have to do with mass production. Think instead of the big tables decorated with beautifully carved rams' heads and acanthus leaves. Lanterns with swags of bronze bellflowers and leafy palmettes. Pedestals and urns painted and carved with dentils, eggs and darts, and fluting. All the same motifs cover mirrors and chairs as well, and most of this enormous body of furniture is perfectly useful in our own rooms today. That, finally, is the point with all this architectural Neoclassical furniture—the fact that it is so easy to use in such a variety of decorative backgrounds.

Using overscale furniture and decorative elements is not treacherous. It just requires a little advance planning. You obviously need an empty wall, and that wall should have a certain centrality about it. We are not talking about pieces that can just be scooted around anywhere. Large entrance halls provide any number of possibilities. A big table, a pair of pedestals, a mirror or two. The same big table that you could use in a large hall would also provide a dramatic focal point in a living room, opposite the fireplace for example, or between a pair of windows. Instead of putting a sofa on the obvious long wall, consider using an imposing piece of real furniture. If there is no fireplace, all the more reason to start the design of the room around something big and rather grand. And if your room is really huge, anchor the whole thing down with a center table or a library table, as many of the great eighteenth-century desks were called. Funnily enough, the excessive richness that frightens so many people where Rococo furniture is concerned is not a problem with Neoclassical furniture. And Kent-style furniture, although very rich, has a particularly muscular quality that prevents it from looking too precious.

Collections of contemporary art and sculpture pose no difficulty when combined with large-scale, architectural furniture. A great side table standing under a large modern canvas looks comfortable with a piece of sculpture on it or a large vase of flowers. Or nothing. A small table needs, in order to justify its existence in a room, something on it. Large, sculptural tables, however, lead lives of their own. I was recently in a room hung entirely with twentieth-century pictures. On one large wall, there was a very big—probably eighty inches long—mahogany side table with a thick white marble top and deep apron carved with typical Adamesque paterae and fluting. A Magritte hung over the table and a Calder stabile stood on top of it. Flanking it were a pair of rather tall pedestals, also decorated with fluting and paterae and still in their old paint. On the pedestals were a pair of Regency lamps in the form of standing Grecian maidens. The whole arrangement was both beautiful and interesting as well as being somewhat original without straining credulity.

Carpets were another fabulous creation of Neoclassical designers. They were filled with the same motifs that were used on furniture of the same period, and we know they were frequently designed to echo the plasterwork on the ceilings of the rooms they were intended for. The orderly, rather geometric arrangement of their patterns once again suits them for contemporary rooms. The coloring of these carpets is often refreshingly vivid, but at the same time the colors are so plentiful that you will find them very unconfining vis-à-vis the selection of today's materials and paint colors.

As the Postmodern style continues developing, it is exciting to contemplate what might be in store for us. More architects seem to be returning to the delights of the past for inspiration and are taking up designing furniture. Meanwhile, as yet another movement inspired by Neoclassicism gains in popularity, those of us who long to live with antiques can look forward to new ways to use them and new surroundings in which to see them. It is wonderfully encouraging to be reminded of the fact that the world of design is never static. There are always at least two alternatives to the present. One is the past, and the other is the future.

THE DELIGHTS
OF CHINOISERIE

To visit Nostell Priory in Yorkshire is a staggering experience. The house was built by John Paine, remodeled by Robert Adam, and, in 1771, supplied with furnishings by Thomas Chippendale. The first impression on entering the state bedroom decorated by Chippendale is the extravagant brilliance of the lacquered chinoiserie furniture. Next to dazzle the eye is the soft faded tonality of the Chinese wallpaper and old chintz at the windows. The gilt Rococo chinoiserie mirror, that bizarre English invention, goes through the roof, so to speak, with a pagoda, birds, palm fronds, and fretwork.

For centuries the Western eye has been delighted by the mysterious East. This fascination began in the late 1200s, when the Venetian Marco Polo came back from China with tales of a splendid and marvelously strange place that almost no other European had seen. In the years to come, first the Spanish and the Portuguese and then the Dutch and the English developed trade routes to the East and began importing Oriental artifacts: textiles, lacquered objects, and porcelain. Because there was such a great demand for the small supply of these unusual and beautiful wares, imitations began to appear in the West. Porcelains were the most popular, and the struggle to discover the secrets of making porcelain in Europe is a saga itself.

The taste for chinoiserie led Europeans at one time or another to decorate every aspect of their houses in a way that evoked the Orient, a place unknown to most people except for representations on brocade, lacquer, wallpaper, and porcelain from the East. In the middle of the eighteenth century a mania for chinoiserie had genuinely taken over as painters and decorators started to fill their worlds with pagodas, bridges, dragons, bells, and exotic birds and flowers. Throughout this fantasy universe pekes and pugs held court and gave tea parties dressed up in long robes and funny hats.

Architects were just as busy ruffling the edges of roofs and enclosing verandas with fretwork balustrades. Chubby Buddhas with nodding heads sat on either side of doorways that were also flanked by Foo dogs. The vocabulary of chinoiserie is amazingly adaptable to nearly anything—a teapot, a curtain valance, a porch column, a garden gate—which accounts for its astonishing prevalence throughout the West.

There isn't a house in the world that wouldn't allow you to indulge in a little Oriental monkey business.

I first came under the spell of the Chinese taste as a child forty years ago when I saw a photograph of the supper room in the Governor's Palace at Colonial Williamsburg. The walls were covered with a beautiful eighteenth-century paper. It had been imported from China by Englishmen two hundred years earlier and was eventually hung in the reconstructed palace. It remained there for half a century until a few years ago, when it was taken down by the curators to reflect more authentically the last royal governor's inventory.

Whether it was authentic to colonial Virginia or not, it was heavenly wallpaper. Painted on a dusky blue background were great gnarled trees and shrubs all sprouting white leaves and flowers shaded in tones of gray. It created a wonderful foil of color and pattern for the room's richly carved white wood-work and vivid yellow damask curtains and swags. The paper did not imitate nature any more than a huge vase of flowers does. It was nature recruited to do the job of delighting the eye and decorating a space, and, as is so often the case, it made no demands on the rest of the room. The chairs and curtains weren't in the least Chinese in feeling. Neither was the cut-glass chandelier. But everything was enhanced by the gorgeous paper. This is another of the compelling aspects of chinoiserie: It is incredibly flexible in its applicability.

One of the most influential voyages to China was that of Sir William Chambers in the 1740s. Chambers was one of England's great architects in a century brimming with architectural genius. He was born in Sweden, where his Scottish parents had settled, and he was only in his teens when he went to China. His book on Chinese design and his later work at Kew Gardens, as well as throughout England, spread a deeper knowledge of Chinese style from furniture to architecture and landscape gardening. Even Frederick the Great commissioned Chambers to design a Chinese bridge for his palace Sanssouci.

Frederick already owned an Oriental fantasy built for him in 1754 by Johann Boüring—a Chinese teahouse that captures the whimsy and freedom

which, along with the beauty, still assures our devotion to chinoiserie. This enchanting pavilion is all curves and arches with golden palm trees for porch columns and a wavy tin roof painted and marbleized in swirls and scrolls. Sitting around the lettuce-green exterior walls are life-size figures of Chinese people who look, thank goodness, like cheerful members of the cast of *The Mikado* rather than the villainous Charlie Chan stereotypes that occasionally spoil the mood of this kind of decoration. The inside of the teahouse is a riot of porcelain, enamels, and painted wallpaper. If you were to see it today in the garden of some chic leader of fashion and society, you would applaud the taste and humor.

Around this time, Frederick's sister, Queen Louisa Ulrica of Sweden, was presented by her husband with a larger and more practical Chinese pavilion that is still one of the main attractions of the gardens of Drottningholm outside Stockholm. This pavilion has the prettiest roof I have ever seen, with undulating waves of tin that make the building look as though it could float

A garden pavilion in Wiltshire based on traditional Italianate features such as the portico and the colonnade took off in another direction when chinoiserie decoration was applied; a moon doorway, a fretwork balustrade. Suddenly a whole new spirit of Chinese whimsy triumphed.

away in the gentlest breeze. Inside it is completely livable, with all the rooms necessary for anyone's happy existence. Many styles are combined with marvelous ease: In addition to chinoiserie, there is Rococo furniture as well as the typical Gustavian versions of Queen Anne and Louis XVI. All the backgrounds, however, make painted and lacquered references to the underlying Chinese theme, and Chinese porcelains of every imaginable shape and color and period are everywhere.

I once saw a room in a Chinese pavilion outside Leningrad in which the window reveals were decorated with pagodas painted in shades of coral red, pale lavender, and pink, with darker tones of brown and green for definition. The room's background, which appeared to be cream-colored wallpaper, was actually wood intarsia in many shades, with ivory used for people's faces. Chinese lacquered pieces and porcelain objects were plentiful, but it was the colorful painted decoration that gave the room its feeling of Oriental fantasy.

The endless variations of the Chinese taste can be used in the architectural details or the furnishings alone—or both together. The greatest monument to chinoiserie is surely the Royal Pavilion at Brighton, which displays every conceivable way that Oriental motifs will enliven a room.

Most of us have vivid images of Brighton's enormous rooms, with their gigantic gilded and lacquered columns and pilasters. But it is in the smaller details of this great *folie* that we see how to apply chinoiserie to contemporary decoration. Wherever you look there are panels of Chinese wallpaper bordered by colored fretwork or slender Chinese columns. Peaked pagoda tops are placed with abandon on overdoors and windows whose valances are edged in bells and finished with scrolls and dragons. Though the juxtaposition of colors is sometimes a little too bold, it is nonetheless exciting: red and black, of course, with lots of gold leaf, but also many shades of pink alongside off-blues and greens that make up backgrounds borrowed directly from the porcelains. Yellows and ochres with darker contrasting shades of brown and red alternate with combinations of pastels in the adjoining spaces. There is such a bombardment of color you are never aware of a single prevailing shade. And that is what prevents the profusion of colors from clashing—there is simply no place for them to clash.

Chinese fantasy decoration will mix well with practically anything else you choose for a room. This quality of being flexible and playful at the same time makes chinoiserie particularly applicable to today's decorating needs. There isn't a house or apartment in the world that wouldn't allow you to indulge in a little Oriental monkey business. Chinese wallpaper fits in equally well with traditional or modern details. It even works with no details, provid-

ing a suitable background against which to place French, English, or contemporary furniture and carpets. The late Pauline Rothschild, a legendary tastemaker in fashion and decoration, had a bedroom with old terra-cotta floor tiles, a bed with bronze posts that resembled Giacometti saplings, Jacobean stools, and panels of Chinese paper set into pagoda-topped frames hung all around the walls, the panels establishing the room's real presence and richness.

In our own era of renewed interest in trompe l'oeil and fancy mural painting, it would be very easy to paint a dado in imitation of Chinese fretwork or to create painted paneling and overdoors based on examples at Brighton. The inexhaustible supply of bamboo-framed furniture offers a broad area of experimentation for all of us who like to paint furniture in exciting colors that would be difficult to work in anywhere else.

I frequently see rooms with a lot of very pretty but clearly second-rate Chinese porcelain. Rather than have it used in an overambitious way, I would much prefer that the scheme include some fanciful chinoiserie wallpaper or paintwork that will lift the serious atmosphere into a lighthearted realm free from the demands of high quality and authenticity. If you have a handsome Coromandel screen that isn't as old or as real as it ought to be, it will look a lot better when treated in an offhand way than if you pretend it is something it is not and make it the focal point of a room. My wife and I have such a screen and it has stood for seventeen years in our entrance hall covering an asymmetrical corner and making no pretensions. Pretentiousness is one thing that should *always* be avoided in decoration, and the appeal of chinoiserie lies to a large extent in its sense of humor.

The Chinese Pavilion at Drottningholm near Stockholm was built in the 1760s and still stands in all its fantastic glory. The building, with a ruffled pagoda roof and dragons spouting bells, appears to defy gravity, while the interior is an experience in color work that prefigures the Royal Pavilion at Brighton. (This building is discussed in greater detail in the chapter that follows.)

A FRESH LOOK
AT BALTIC STYLES

I often think that today we lack originality as far as design is concerned, that our time is noteworthy for an absence rather than a presence of memorable new furniture styles. There is, of course, all that avant-garde furniture that seems to come from Milan, but how many people do you know who actually live with that look? Are we stagnant? Uninspired? I wonder.

But then I think of all the formerly neglected styles that have been revived and are now popular, and it occurs to me that perhaps this is the important design contribution of the present era. Our understanding of the taste of other periods, our sensitivity to historical design is far deeper and more widespread now than it was even fifteen or twenty years ago.

One area of the decorative arts that is more appreciated now than it was just a few years ago is the whole category of northern European, or Baltic, decoration. From Scandinavia across into Russia, there existed from the second half of the eighteenth century to well into the nineteenth a succession of design movements that were a vigorous and creative response to what was going on in other parts of Europe at the time. With a great deal of subtlety and originality, Scandinavian and Russian furniture makers translated the taste of England, France, Germany, and Italy into a language of their own.

What the northern Europeans created always possessed a certain wayward quality that distinguished these interpretations from their original inspirations. What makes the present design climate remarkable is that we admire this quirkiness and recognize in it the charm that, although always there, was for so long overlooked.

There are basically two schools of design that left their marks on this Northern furniture. One is Rococo and the other is Neoclassical. The first to

In Jan and Merrill Stenbeck's
17th-century farmhouse near
Stockholm one of the guest rooms
contains white-painted Gustavian
furniture, gauze-draped windows,
and printed cotton bed covers.
The floors are scrubbed pine and
the wall planks are painted
blue gray. The colors of the room,
so typically Swedish, are those
of air and water.

appear, as was true throughout Europe, was the Rococo style. The perfect example of fanciful Northern Rococo is the Chinese Pavilion at Drottningholm, the Swedish royal palace. Dating from the 1760s, this marvelous building still exists in all its glory, and it is an enchanting example of the play between the imported taste of the time and the amusing twist given this taste by its Swedish interpreters.

Inside this lovely Chinese-style building, beyond the ruffled pagoda roof with its bells dangling from the mouths of dragons, is a range of furniture styles that spans the European taste of the time. The decoration tells us volumes about people of fashion everywhere in the late eighteenth century. It also tells a lot about the Scandinavian genius for color and light.

The strange, forbidding climate of the Far North has had the positive effect of teaching the people who live there the value of these two visual qualities—qualities that in addition to pleasing the eye lift the spirit. For example, there are rooms in this fantasy retreat at Drottningholm that are painted vermilion red with black-and-gold lacquer panels and furniture with gilded frames and bright red covers. Other rooms are peacock blue with emerald green and gold decorations and black lacquer chairs, or forest green with hot pink panels outlined in gold leaf, or egg-yolk yellow with red-and-black japanned panels. Imagine all of this going on before the Royal Pavilion at Brighton even existed!

Some of the furniture at Drottningholm was made in Paris, the nerve center of the fashion world. Other pieces, however, have the unmistakable look of Swedish furniture. Painted chairs abound in a sort of Queen Anne style, but they have odd knees on the legs and strange feet, and they are always fanciful. The combination is provincial and sophisticated at the same time.

What this prodigious design statement was leading to was the Gustavian era that came with the last quarter of the century—the culmination of the light, airy, cottony rooms that a small coterie has loved ever since, and that all of us love now.

Gustavus III, the son of the builders of the Chinese Pavilion, was one of history's meteoric creatures whose talent and glitter refuse to die, although these sparkling people often die young. Poor Gustavus was assassinated at forty-six, but his immortal legend was well established before then.

Gustavus was a great student, a brilliant writer (the Swedish theater was virtually created by him), and an altogether unforgettable fellow. As a very young man, he was tutored by the great statesmen of his day, one of whom was the son of Tessin, the extraordinary Swedish architect whose own father had also been a great architect. As a youthful emissary to France, Gustavus was the hit of Paris. He also adored French taste, although who in the world could have resisted it in the 1770s?

Gustavian furniture and decoration possessed a clean simplicity and spontaneity that is especially appealing to us. Rooms in light colors, mixtures of gilded, painted, and natural wood furniture covered in simple, cozy cotton materials convey an unpretentious atmosphere that comes as a relief to those of us who love period decoration but dread being stifled by too much richness.

The Gustavian style moved naturally into the next phase of European taste—Neoclassicism. It could be said that the requirements of manufacture render the Rococo style one of the most challenging areas of the decorative arts. Refinement, delicacy, and grace—characteristics of the Rococo—more often than not elude the provincial craftsman. Occasionally, a crudely made fauteuil or mirror frame with naïve C-scrolls has great appeal. More often, however, a lack of finesse in Rococo work causes disastrous results. Remote country wood-carvers and cabinetmakers did not face the same problems with the plainer Neoclassical style. In addition, the more disciplined classical vocabulary seems to have had a very lasting appeal to the Northern mind as well as the Northern eye.

In Russia, the Baroque architecture of Rastrelli and Quarengi, early transplants from Italy, was rich and florid enough for any despot, but for some reason it did not last very long in that part of the world. When the vogue for ancient Greek and Roman taste captured the fancy of the Western World, it found a special home in the land of the midnight sun and thrived there with vigor for the next forty or fifty years. That's a long lifespan in the fickle world of taste, don't you agree? Catherine the Great's Scottish architect, Charles Cameron, was one of those people who appear now and then, create a few masterpieces, and slip into the shadows of history. Cameron seems to have absorbed everything that the Adam movement and the ruins of Rome had to offer.

In the 1770s, Cameron began to build Pavlovsk, a perfect Neoclassical palace, for Catherine's son Paul and his wife, Maria Feodorovna. This unhappy pair (Paul was eventually stabbed and trampled to death by a group of shall we say dissatisfied subjects) had just produced a son and heir, and Pavlovsk was their reward for this successful act. Cameron's heavenly palace, which looks like a Palladian villa, possesses more chic and glamour than you can imagine. And like a lot of the architecture and decoration of this part of the world, Pavlovsk evokes about four different countries and cultures. There is an enormous amount of decoration that reminds one of the sumptuous houses Robert Adam designed and decorated in England and Scotland. There are echoes of France, from the Louis XVI style of the Petit Trianon to the later style of Ledoux with its extremes of detail. There are signs of Imperial Rome everywhere, and finally references to ancient Egypt. If this sounds like a banana split, I have misled you. It is a triumph of decoration and architecture, and it is built on a sensible scale rare in Russia that makes it appealing to our twentieth-century eye.

Pavlovsk's fanciful, sometimes extreme furniture is equally varied in its references. Many of the chairs teeter between the English Regency and contemporaneous Italian styles. There are also clear signs of the movement toward the unconventional, very architectural shapes that became a characteristic of fancy Baltic furniture—desks and cabinets surmounted by pediments and domes and supported on numerous legs shaped like columns—forms not unlike those of the later, Biedermeier period, another style popular in the North.

The paradoxical ease with which the rich style of Robert Adam could be translated into a simple vernacular is exemplified by the romantic little summer house in Denmark called Liselund that was built in the 1790s. It also illustrates the crosscurrents of taste. The garden is laid out in the naturalistic way then newly fashionable in England. Yet the exterior of the house is simple whitewashed brick with a humble thatched cottage roof and porch columns made of the simplest possible posts.

Inside there are many surprises. The decoration is extremely sophisticated, but the execution is lighthearted and underdone. There is an absence of actual architectural detailing; instead, that is all achieved by trompe l'oeil. Marbleized floors, Ionic pilasters, niches with urns of flowers in them, Chinese fretwork panels—everything is painted in an almost casual way. The furniture is a combination of styles. Some of it follows the designs of Hepplewhite. Other pieces resemble Louis XVI or Directoire models. All of it is painted and fresh-looking. If the word *timeless* can ever be used, it clearly describes this pale, scrubbed-looking house.

The most timeless of all interpreters of style, particularly Swedish style, was the painter Carl Larsson (1853-1919), whose paintings of his own

Today the wayward charm of Scandanavian design is recognized by nearly everyone.

interiors were a sensation when they were first seen at the turn of the century. With his wife, Karin, he created a country house that has been a museum since his death—and, really, a shrine to an artist's simple decoration that is nevertheless rich in details and historical allusions.

These unforgettable little rooms are full of light and comfort. They display an unabashed love of prettiness. Pots of flowers stand in windows with starchy gauze valances. Delicate white painted chairs sport blue-and-white cotton covers that have a loose, homemade look that appeals to all of us who admire the evidence of handwork in a room. There are pillows everywhere. The scrubbed floors are sparingly spread with rag runners. Painted decorations, usually in the form of flowers but often small portraits, appear on doors and cornices and cupboards.

Then there are the colors themselves: clear yellows and greens used in conjunction with bright blue and white. And, finally, Larsson's famous Swedish red—a warm coral color. The cozy informality that we all pride ourselves on, that quality of manners that is the opposite of pomposity, becomes a visual phenomenon in these Swedish rooms. It is as much a sociological legacy as it is an aesthetic one. It is a uniquely Northern style that at the same time draws on all parts of Europe. Naturally, it looks wonderful in any part of the world.

Liselund is a severe and romantic Neoclassical summer house built in Denmark in 1792 by the architect Andreas Kirkerup and a pair of aristocratic clients who refused his Greek temple sketches. They insisted on a thatched roof. Inside, all the decoration—marble floors and walls, pilasters, shell carving —is trompe l'oeil.

LEARNING FROM THE
ENGLISH COUNTRY HOUSE

*This is my best recollection
of Earlywood, a house near Ascot
where the Dowager Countess
of Portarlington lived. This very
English setting included Chinese
and Korean antiquities, William
Kent tables, French chairs, English
18th-century portraits in their
original frames, sisal carpeting,
books, magazines, ashtrays, drinks
supplies—all done in a subtle
color scheme.*

When American magazine editors describe rooms as being done up in the English country-house style, they usually mean the Colefax & Fowler style, which has developed over the past thirty or forty years into a look characterized by a palette of clear colors and paintwork stippled or dragged in a strié pattern along with passages of marbleizing and trompe l'oeil. These light, easy rooms usually have curtains and valances made of chintz and trimmed with fringe and ruffles and bows. The furniture consists of comfortable upholstered pieces combined with antiques in mahogany as well as painted and gilded finishes from several periods of the eighteenth and nineteenth centuries.

More often than not, these interpretations of the original and now legendary Colefax & Fowler rooms possess a delicate feminine quality that contradicts the masculinity of the deeply comfortable rooms they are imitating: rooms with old worn carpets and turn-of-the-century upholstered furniture which, instead of being newly reupholstered, is covered in loose slipcovers that look (and perhaps are) homemade. There are books everywhere and leather club fenders in front of smoke-streaked mantelpieces. This is commonly called the undecorated look. Sometimes it is the result of happenstance; sometimes a subtle effort has been made to design a timeworn atmosphere.

Whether they are decorated or not is beside the point. There have always been some English rooms that were decorated from head to toe. The English country-house style, however, refers to a spiritual as well as a visual style. The spirit of English decorating is rooted in a veneration for the real past (their houses, after all, are often occupied by the same family for generations) and in a firm belief that newness is vulgar and fashion is to be disregarded. All of this is, of course, the essence of reverse snobbery, which is the hallmark of the style.

Another example of pure Englishness is the library-drawing room in the dower house at Badminton where the Duke and Duchess of Beaufort lived. Its chintz slipcovers, Oriental rug, Chinese lamps, swagged curtains, plants and flowers everywhere are part of an atmosphere of comfort and relaxed living.

The spirit of English decorating is rooted in a veneration for the past and a firm belief that newness is vulgar.

An article in *House & Garden* once described the former sitting room of David and Lady Caroline Somerset (now the Duke and Duchess of Beaufort) as the quintessential English room. This terribly inviting space combined the functions of a library with those of a drawing room. It really was what we Americans call a living room. The bookcases, which ran all around the room, went from floor to ceiling and were decorated with slender pilasters and topped by a large cornice that formed a uniform crown molding throughout. The rich parchment color of the walls and woodwork evolved from an off-white chimney breast discolored by smoke from the fireplace. The gently arched French windows were curtained in a soft green material hung from rings and poles; attached swags were heavily fringed.

The Somersets' furniture was covered in a variety of materials, some pieces in rose-flowered chintz with red wool fringe and red cording, others in shades of red or a light mole color or old needlework. The patterned Oriental carpet had a soft red background. A mahogany pedestal desk was loaded with writing materials. There was a basket piled three feet high with firewood. Postcards and invitations were strewn along the mantel shelf under a dashing portrait. In this case, we can be sure that the portrait represented a family relation and had not been found in an antique shop. Potted plants and cut flowers of every sort added to the clutter and pattern of the magazines and books that filled the room.

Although I never saw this often-photographed room, I know its successor well, the current library at Badminton where the duke and duchess now live. It is another version of the quintessential English room. Although Badminton is a fabled house that was worked on by both William Kent and James Gibbs, the library, in spite of its great height and splendid dark paneling, is a room of perfect coziness.

Some of the furniture from the previous sitting room has found its way there, still in its old chintz covers. Other pieces have been covered in a new chintz with colors soft enough to melt into the rich tones of the paneling and book bindings without *looking* new. A gigantic green velvet ottoman covered with neat piles of magazines sits in front of the fireplace, and the curtains, also green, resemble the old ones. On easels in front of the bookcases are twin eighteenth-century views of the house and park painted by Canaletto. A nice souvenir from the past! Around the top of the tall room hangs a row of portraits. The mood, without a breath of stateliness, is a romantic vision of life in a great house set in a vast English park. The whole atmosphere is an inspired background for living.

Some rooms are unfortunately all *foreground,* with pictures and accessories jumping out at you, extravagant flowers, rich effects. Collections of what auction catalogs label "rare" and "extremely fine" furniture cause you to ponder ghastly questions such as how much all this must have cost. A general feeling of intimidation sets in. At the very heart of the English country-house room, though, there is a sense of a welcoming *background*—for reading and writing, for physical as well as visual comfort. It is a background appealing to men and women alike, to cityfolk and countryfolk, to grownups and children. The fire crackles away (and smokes sometimes too); the promise of tea is actually kept, and when the tea tray arrives there is something delicious to eat on it.

The simple English farmhouse sitting close to the ground with its paneled hall and the sort of staircase that resembles our own colonial versions is another architectural type that is very pleasing to the modern eye. One of my favorite examples is in Oxfordshire and is still surrounded by its farm buildings. The entrance drive goes past barns and sheds and an old orchard. The main part of the house is early eighteenth century, but there are later wings and additions, including a library built just a few years ago.

The front door is almost level with the motor court, which allows you to enter without any undue sense of grandeur. What you do feel upon entering is a close connection to the garden and surrounding farm. In the hall you see boots and hats, baskets and leashes. The table has a well-worn visitors' book, a bowl of flowers, a pretty dish that usually has a set of car keys in it. Because the floors are old and irregular, a flat small-patterned carpet covers everything and

Here are three hundred years of decorative artifacts assembled forty years ago in a way that would completely suit today's taste: Regency cabinet, 17th-century portrait, small-patterned fitted carpet, highly polished Georgian silver. This was the Hon. David Herbert's dining room at his cottage in the park at Wilton.

goes on up the stairs. The Queen Anne paneling, which once was painted, has been stripped and waxed. A pair of mirrors, far too rich for the architecture and proportions of the house but beautiful nevertheless, hangs over bookcases that hold the overflow of books and magazines.

In the small rooms you pass through on your way to the big new library there are many pieces of attractive furniture—none of which seems to have been recently acquired, all of which I would love to own. The sofas and chairs are covered in lovely materials, with a certain amount of the inevitable chintz, but nowhere does there appear to be a rigid scheme. The library has two cozy seating groups in addition to a desk, a drinks table, a gaming table, and about eight small chairs that can be moved wherever they are needed. The pictures span two hundred years, and their differing market values are equally widespread. Furniture comes and goes along with the books and flowers, but there is no sense of impermanence. Every part of this house reverberates with the liveliness of family life and farm activity.

On a grander note, I have wonderful memories of a house in Yorkshire. This tall pedimented brick house, known as Sutton Park, resembles in its severity some American houses of the eighteenth century. Mrs. Sheffield, the woman who lives there, has a deep interest in interior decoration and gardening; the undecorated look is not something that concerns her. In the little dining room near her front door on walls intricately painted in faux tortoiseshell hangs a collection of Imari porcelain. A small sitting room contains French furniture and elaborate silk curtains and valances. Off this room a large high-ceilinged drawing room is decorated with antique Chinese wallpaper and a large number of beautiful English antiques.

Upstairs there are a lot of romantically feminine bedrooms, most with four-poster beds finished with complicated canopies of chintz and silk taffeta. At the foot of each of these beds stands a writing table equipped with the implements of the epistolary art. Chaise longues, fireplaces with mirrored overmantels, and pretty pictures and objects delight the eye and make one glad to be staying there. No corner of this marvelous establishment, including the garden, I might add, is uninviting; and, as is so often the case in English houses, the library heads the list of places where one wants to be. Seen at the end of the entrance hall the moment you enter, this warmly paneled room is filled with light, which is intensified by the golden yellows and rich browns of the needlework and the materials covering the furniture. It is both the architectural and ceremonial focus of the house, occupying the center of attention from the moment you step in the front door.

The way you enter many English country houses is in itself an embodiment of the style. In many houses with overpoweringly grand entrances, you generally use a side door into a hall that contains all sorts of signs of people, dogs, and horses. It isn't exactly a mud room, but it certainly is informal. The prevailing atmosphere is not stifling and hushed in a way that makes you feel like a clumsy intruder whose presence is a flaw in an otherwise perfect setting. I feel miserable in terrifyingly grand houses where I want to remain standing when the rigid butler offers me a seat in a tomblike salon. What I love best of all is to enter a house with some beautiful architectural detail (even if it's only the doorway), to see handsome furniture along with the umbrellas and walking sticks, even a coat or two if the closet is not nearby, to notice that the doorknobs are brightly polished even if the paint on the woodwork is faded and old, to look ahead into a room that beckons welcomingly with comfortable chairs and lots of books, and to smell the mingled perfumes of flowers, fires, and fresh air.

Twenty-five years ago I saw a heavenly house that had been decorated twenty years before that by Syrie Maugham for the Dowager Countess of Portarlington, a creature of incredible taste. The house was big but not particularly beautiful. Inside, its Victorian incrustations had been stripped away and replaced with details more Georgian in character. The large entrance hall was an immediate tip-off that something marvelous was going on. The walls were glazed the color of corn, and the floor was covered with coarse rush matting. The pictures were eighteenth-century portraits in good gilt frames. There was a big William Kent console table with flowers and a drinks tray flanked by a pair of Coromandel screens. Huge Régence chairs were covered in beige linen. On the floor stood baskets, some filled with wood and some filled with magazines. Gigantic Korean pots contained blooming trees from the greenhouse. And the fire was blazing away.

This house had everything—a feeling of informal comfort as well as chic, an atmosphere of luxury that was not indecent. It had a personality that reflected its owner's taste. Is that too much to ask of a house? We know it can be done because thousands of English people have achieved it for generations, and that is why we emulate the way they live—not just the way they decorate. They *inhabit* their houses, along with their children and their pets, their collections and their guests. They are an inspiration.

EARLY AMERICAN PURITY

In the decorating annals of the United States, the longest-running show is Early American. It is a beloved thread that runs through our history without a break. If there were an Academy Award for design, the Oscar would have to take the form of a Windsor chair.

My earliest recollections of New England farmhouses consist of a blur of Hollywood images that I now know were simply ridiculous. They still delight me, though, whenever they reappear on the screen. My favorite is the house in *Holiday Inn* with its fieldstone fireplaces and bogus Connecticut River valley paneling. These houses always had beams, and windows with about fifty panes, and dozens of steps leading to the various rooms, no two of which seemed to be on the same level—and, Windsor chairs and puffy quilted chintz. It was all adorable. So was the lady of the house—and she invariably wore an apron.

My first real experience with Early American decoration was the farmhouse of my parents' best friend, Cornelia Hadley, an enchanting figure from my childhood in Indiana, who along with my mother had the best taste in town. With her combined love of painting and antiquing—the latter an addiction of my parents and the former an addiction of mine—Cornelia was our constant companion whether shopping or sitting on camp stools painting in the middle of a field.

My favorite memories, however, are of Cornelia in her house on Route 40 where she had grown up. This simple farmhouse had been moved back when the road was widened in the 1930s. Its porches and bits of gingerbread trim were removed, and with the addition of dark green shutters and a big stone chimney, the house had taken on an earlier, less Victorian appearance. The real transformation, however, took place inside.

This chair displayed at the Winterthur Museum has the beautifully shaped frame characteristic of the Queen Anne style and the simple cylindrical back legs characteristic of the Philadelphia version of that style.

White walls were a bold decorating statement forty years ago, at least in rural Indiana. In those days rooms were painted or papered in soft, often dull shades of unexciting colors like old rose and sandalwood. Cornelia bravely painted her walls dead white—the color of plaster. The wide old floorboards were good to begin with, and they were finished a rich natural color, not too dark and not too light. The walnut mantel in the living room was stripped down to its natural color, then waxed and polished. On it stood a fine mahogany clock and tall brass candlesticks and a stupendous pair of dueling pistols.

There were bookcases filled entirely with books, and my first copy of *Catcher in the Rye* came from those shelves. All the upholstered furniture was slipcovered, and over the biggest sofa hung an Audubon print of blue jays (one of the birds was invading an egg, but to all of us children he appeared to be blowing bubble gum). The star attraction of the room was a twelve-foot-square hooked rug made by Cornelia over a long period of time. It was composed of alternating squares of flowers and octagons, the octagons made of gray-and-white work socks which gave them the softly speckled quality of spongeware.

Most old farmhouses were planned to economize on space, which means, among other things, that they have few hallways—you look from one room into the next. The views through Cornelia's house were of old pewter buffed to a lovely shine, collections of ironstone, old maps applied directly onto the walls like wallpaper, and four-poster beds with antique quilts and starched pillow shams and dust ruffles. All the rugs were handmade. The windows had wood Venetian blinds or shutters and simple unlined muslin curtains trimmed with cotton fringe. Electrified candlesticks and Sandwich glass oil lamps provided light.

There was nothing stuffy or serious about Cornelia's house. The mood, although chaste and simple, was achieved with a variety of pieces from different periods of the eighteenth and nineteenth centuries, as is usually the case in a family house going back many generations. Rather than emphasize the differences between the periods, the spare quality of the rooms unified the many modest elements in a fresh way. I suppose any bold means used throughout a house tends to unify it.

One of the most compelling aspects of Early American decorating is its willingness to accept pieces from other periods as long as the spirit of Americana is maintained. Variety has always been central to the style. Three hundred years ago no one was fussy about a correct interpretation of any one period. The earliest Americans used whatever was available, and they were grateful for it too, I'll bet. What made the style beautiful then and what interests us about it now is its simplicity and its sense of Puritanical discipline.

Throughout history, many colonial styles have been corrupt—too big, too ornate, too crude. Think of the British raj, think of Roman outposts in North Africa. But the tough, devout dissenters who underwent punishing hardships to survive in the New World gave birth to a tradition of decoration that is unusual because of its stoic beauty. And being the offshoot of a society that was moving into its greatest period of aesthetic achievement was obviously a piece of good fortune.

When I was fourteen years old, lying about my age to get in, I went to see the Winterthur Museum in Delaware. It was one of the great epiphanies of my life, one which is repeated each time I return. I wish I could go into elaborate detail about this remarkable house and the equally remarkable personality of its creator, Henry Francis du Pont, a man of great taste and knowledge who also had the vision and perfectionism that the very rich could indulge many years ago.

My complete list of favorite rooms at Winterthur is too long to enumerate, but the ones that have a permanent place in my memory are filled with color and decoration. Although it is strict and pure, there is no chill at Winterthur. In the Queen Anne Dining Room, for example, there are low ceilings and typically restrained but lovely paneling painted grass green. A drop-leaf table is surrounded by a collection of shapely Queen Anne chairs covered in a large-scale blue-and-white resist-dye pattern. There is blue-and-white delft, some including mauve. A big paneled cupboard has its doors wide open, and more delft is inside.

One of Henry Francis du Pont's favorite color ranges was blue to green. Some of his deep-colored rooms tend to look a little more green, while others, like his bedroom with its superb paneling, tend to be a little more blue. I find these subtle but strong shades unequaled in their ability to tie together the rich tones of Oriental carpets, old earthenware, and woods of all sorts. Antique textiles in indigo blues and the odd reds that vegetable dyes yielded can be killed by the use of too many modern, clear colors in their vicinity. On the other hand, these old materials can become stuffy and dull when linked with too much brown and beige, which many collectors and decorators choose as the proper neutral accompaniment. The blue green colors of colonial America, however, are not only refreshing and authentic, but they also serve as a far better neutral background.

In addition to all the primitive elements of Early American design at Winterthur, there are numerous examples of grander decoration that remind us of the astonishing achievement of our forefathers—particularly their ability to adapt the highest forms of Georgian design for their own practical purposes. To me, Winterthur's Philadelphia rooms are remarkably beautiful. There are carvings and shapes that become more original and fascinating the more you look at them. The back legs of the chairs alone—those simple cylinders—are enough to tell you that they represent a strong point of view.

Another world-famous landmark of Early American design is Colonial Williamsburg, in Virginia. In addition to the gorgeous reconstructions the Rockefellers built when they restored the colonial capital in the 1930s, numerous houses of the eighteenth century survive. The Peyton-Randolph and Brush-Everard houses are perfect examples of the latter. One of the bedrooms tucked under the gable of the Brush-Everard house could serve as the inspiration for almost any attic room today. The walls and ceilings are all part of a continuous surface of changing planes, painted plaster white. A version of the green blue I have been talking about is used on the woodwork. Natural wood Venetian blinds hang at the uncurtained windows, blending with the many wood colors of the scrubbed pine floor, the bedsteads, the highboy, and the Chippendale chairs. Blue appears again on the coarsely stitched coverlets, and white is repeated in the starched muslin of the dressing table. Touches of brass, blue-and-white delft, and a couple of raspberry chair seats finish off a color scheme of great subtlety, paradoxically warm given the cool elements that make it up.

Enthusiasts of Early American design are able to choose today from a vast array of antiques and reproductions offering every conceivable artifact that was or might have been made in colonial America. The trouble with all this commerciality and fakery is the obvious joke it has made Early American taste seem to those who are unsympathetic. Badly made maple spice racks containing philodendron plants and phony coffee grinders turned into lamps are beside the point. The real spirit of the period, whether embodied in a bombé bureau-bookcase from Boston or a mule-eared chair from Lancaster, will always prevail over the onslaught of plastic and chipboard in American life.

Over the past couple of years I have been working on a new house on the ocean in Florida. It belongs to people who love American furniture and whose most treasured possessions are a number of formal eighteenth-century Newport pieces from the great period of Goddard and Townsend. For their vacation retreat, however, they wanted an atmosphere of openness and informality and even a little whimsy.

The house is full of rag rugs and crude tables and chairs from Pennsylvania and New England, many of which are painted in odd shades of blue and green and reddish brown. A particular pair of peacock blue Shaker rocking chairs (now faded and distressed) became the point of departure for a whole

range of painted objects and furniture that, collected together and surrounded by the brilliance of the ocean and the Florida skies, give the house a delightful and totally American feeling of country charm and simplicity. The highly polished terra-cotta tiles of the floors and the crudely whitewashed ceiling beams are in complete harmony with the wood tones and the colors of all that lighthearted painted furniture. Nothing is too simple or too informal to fit in.

Where we had to use new furniture, we applied painted finishes, intentionally worked over to fit in with the old ones. Collections of old earthenware in sponged glazes and bits of terra-cotta and glass blend together in an effortless way. The longevity of Early American style is the result of this capacity to absorb a large variety of objects, both humble and precious, crude and refined, in rooms that appeal to our love of antiques and old-fashioned decoration.

The Early American rooms we create can be just as strict and spare as we want them to be. They do not, however, have to be stiff and uncomfortable. I am sure those tight-lipped Puritans with their marvelous taste and their lofty morals would keel over if they saw an ersatz dry sink made of knotty pine, but I'm glad their legacy has continued over the centuries. In spite of the transgressions and bastardizations that clutter the shopping malls of America, the wonderful world of Early American decoration is as incorruptible as the zealots who created it.

The William Card house, built in Newport, Rhode Island, in 1811, is an example of the classic clapboard New England design that has been adapted for the past two hundred years in America. Although it includes many of the strict elements of Early American architecture, the off-center doorway shows how freely those elements can be employed.

Plans

HOW TO CREATE
INTERIOR VIEWS

This suite at the Munich Residenz was designed for the Bavarian royal family in the 18th century by Cuvilliés in his exuberant Rococo style. Here one can experience the ultimate in interior views, also known as enfilades, which are rooms strung along like beads on a thread. The beauty and the sense of anticipation such interflowing floor plans create must explain why the time-honored axial relationship of rooms— abandoned in the 19th century—is coming back into favor.

If wandering through suites of rooms at Versailles and Schönbrunn and Chatsworth delights your eye, then the side trips from major capitals that take a few hours or a few days are justified, but the reasons for looking at serious, formal architecture are practical as well as pleasurable. Our National Gallery's famous 1986 exhibition devoted to the treasures of English houses certainly awakened many people to the richness and complexity of this sort of establishment over the past several centuries. Repeated visits to the rooms themselves, however, allow for more than the delicious historic and aesthetic fantasies that many of us indulged in at the museum in Washington. A visit to a great house reveals a number of plain truths that have to do with architecture and building as well as with decoration, and these truths are often not perceived by looking at photographs, reading floor plans, or looking at flat elevation drawings. You must actually be in the rooms from time to time to get a feeling for them. Sooner or later, an awful lot of us end up having to make changes of a structural nature to the rooms we live in or to the new rooms we are planning to move into, and here is where all this soaking up of architecture comes in handy.

You don't have to be poor John Ruskin standing on a ladder measuring the distances between columns either. I am just talking about some very obvious things that can be overlooked if not pointed out, or that can be misinterpreted due to the ancientness or grandeur of the examples in question. Universal practices that have worked for hundreds of years often come from a very simple lexicon. These architectural ploys can be applied to the planning of practically all rooms and are particularly useful in the remodeling of existing houses and apartments. We think of decoration as the surface way to finish or improve a room. Often in the process of decorating, however, if you incorpo-

consider the aesthetic pleasure of looking through a doorway and seeing a painterly view of the rooms beyond.

Enfilades existed in modest houses as well as royal palaces, as this illustration shows. I borrowed the interior from a genre painting by Emanuel de Witte, the 17th-century Dutch artist who painted churches as well as bourgeois houses. As in any good enfilade, the doorway details and the play of light and shadow delight the eye.

rate certain architectural adjustments, you can achieve a finished result that goes a great deal further than decorating alone.

The color illustration, an enfilade of rooms in the Munich Residenz looking from a bedroom designed by Cuvilliés through a suite of four more rooms and out a window, might not seem to make much sense vis-à-vis present-day life, but it is precisely this lining up of doorways that often plays such an important part in the entire relationship of adjoining rooms. The word *enfilade* means strung along like beads on a thread, and for centuries, it was the way rooms were arranged in houses both grand and simple.

There are several reasons why this approach to room connection lost favor among architects and their patrons. First, probably, is the question of privacy, and not only privacy among the members of the family. In the nineteenth century, large houses began to fill up with even more servants than before, and the need to feel secluded was, no doubt, very great. Advances in heating and the consequent demand for more of this great comfort certainly affected the future of the airy (probably drafty) enfilade. And finally, there was the age-old element of changing fashion. It was considered an outmoded way to build. The nineteenth-century love of multiplicity and complexity is evident in the plans of houses as well as in their ornamentation. There are, I am sure, other reasons as well, but one thing is certain: These reasons for doing away with long vistas had a lasting effect on the way many houses were built for years. None of the reasons is particularly relevant today.

The critical thing to remember or to relearn is, I feel, the fact that this open, axial relationship of doors to doors and doors to windows is neither simply old-fashioned nor is it a characteristic only of pompous interior spaces. There are tremendous advantages involved. Consider, first of all, the aesthetic pleasure of looking from one room through a doorway to another, and seeing a very painterly view of the next room or rooms. Your anticipation of the space beyond is both heightened and prolonged by this view. And if the doors are placed near windows, the richness of the varied surfaces and textures is particularly apparent. The framed light falling across a polished floor in one room and onto a carpet in the next or highlighting the moldings and paintwork of the receding spaces creates a pictorial view with a focus and composition that far surpasses that of a dead end leading nowhere.

When you consider Dutch interior paintings of the seventeenth century, you can easily appreciate the fact that this shadowbox effect can be delightful in the humblest of situations. Pieter de Hooch's enchanting pictures dwell on the most ordinary of locations—looking through a sitting room to a bedroom, or from a kitchen out onto a paved yard. The sense of promise in the still life seen in the distance, however, belies the simplicity or the predictableness of the actual room beyond.

The harmonious linking of decorative schemes takes on an added importance when you view them together in succession. This clearheaded approach to the progression of color from one room to the next has been practiced for years by many of the greatest decorators who, instead of decorating rooms as they come, moved doors and windows and fireplaces in order to get the room right prior to moving ahead with the problems of decorating. Mrs. Archibald Brown at McMillen spent half a century clarifying the floor plans of the numberless houses and apartments that fell into her sphere, and it was, as we all know, a very large sphere. She also left a lasting stamp on many of her followers. It would be very easy to imagine Albert Hadley, who worked for several years with Mrs. Brown, moving a doorway four inches to get it into the proper alignment. That this sense of axis and order is to a large extent innate is illustrated by Albert's wonderful anecdote dealing with his early childhood

In remodeling the guest suite of a Long Island farmhouse, I was able to create an enfilade from the bedroom through the dressing room to the bathroom by moving the doorways. A minimum of three rooms is needed for the processional effect.

when he threatened to run away from home unless his father had their driveway rebuilt to form a circle centered on the façade of the house. I believe the driveway was in fact changed.

A perfect example of what can be achieved through remodeling is the house in San Francisco that belongs to Tony Hail, another famous decorator steeped in classical traditions. Built in the 1860s, the house was first remodeled in 1916 by Julia Morgan, the architect for the Hearst family who designed San Simeon. Miss Morgan converted the façade to that of a miniature Italianate villa. The interior, although redesigned, was planned with many halls and passageways, all of which were either eliminated or realigned by Tony in the late seventies. Furthermore, *every* door in the entire house was made to line up with one or more other doors. Finally, this system of doorways is on axis with the windows. This unbelievably strict discipline has resulted in groups of rooms that provide the perfect spatial environment for his collections of furniture, objects, carpets, and pictures. These marvelous Hail collections are themselves very coherent—French, Danish, and Swedish furniture primarily from the period of Louis XVI, pale Persian and Samarkand carpets, lightly toned Oriental porcelain and earthenware, and a wealth of drawings and paintings dealing mostly with architectural subjects.

Where hallways have been eliminated, the sacrifice is not that terrible. Halls, after all, unless they are fairly large, can be very dead spaces. How much livelier to be in a place capable of containing furniture that has to do with the comforts of sitting and reading.

On a less lofty plane, but equally enjoyable to my family and me, is a tiny gardener's cottage we remodeled and enlarged for ourselves a few years ago. The work involved extending the kitchen and, at the opposite end of the house, adding on a new entrance hall and living room. Starting with the far wall of the living room, which faces south, there is a wide French window; opposite the window and centered on it is a double-width opening to the entrance hall. Opposite that opening are two steps leading up to the dining room, which is entered through an identical opening also on the same center line. Still on center, continuing on the far side of the dining room, are doors leading into the pantry and directly on out to the kitchen. At last, and with the same center axis, is a kitchen window and an old maple tree outside. The total distance is a little over 80 feet—the extreme length of the house. The effect is light, certainly very convenient and comfortable. The distant views with the changing shadows, shafts of sunlight, and the resultant nuances of color give enormous pleasure.

I was recently taken through a ravishing enfilade of rooms in a great house in Paris. At the end of the vista hung an Ingres portrait. As we walked from room to room, pausing to look at the wonders that were everywhere, the Ingres portrait continued to catch the eye. Each glimpse enhanced the pleasure that was in store. The same is true of my maple tree, or of one of de Hooch's views into a tile-floored kitchen. Privacy does not need to be sacrificed. Central heating keeps us too hot most of the time, and I can't remember any recent complaints about too many servants. All in all, as in the case of many building practices deeply rooted in the past, it seems to me like a pretty good way to arrange rooms.

FURNITURE PLACEMENT THAT MAKES A LIVING ROOM WORK

The drawing room at Casa Amesti in Monterey, California, was designed by Frances Elkins in the late forties but it can still be viewed as a case study in successful room arranging. The plan of the space is very symmetrical and would work with any style of furniture. One long wall includes a fireplace; opposite stands a row of French windows leading to a balcony. A large Georgian partners' desk holds the center of the room. There are seating groups of several sizes with small chairs to pull up wherever they are needed.

When we think of comfort, we often boil the whole issue down to whether a chair is just right or a lighting fixture makes reading easy or the television set is in a good place. These are no doubt important considerations, but the larger view of comfort involves far more. The job of getting a room to work comfortably is often fairly complicated. Frequently the real challenge, which requires knowledge and experience in addition to an "eye," is the arrangement of a room.

In rooms dedicated to the pleasure of a single person, namely private studies, the problems of arrangement are not troublesome. Some of the most charming rooms to look at, both in art and in books on the history of decoration, are those very intimate inner sanctums that can be luxurious and quirky and redolent of personal taste. The most plentiful and delicious of all these depictions, in my opinion, are the pictures of the sublime Madame de Pompadour exquisitely dressed and surrounded by a superb clutter of objects she commissioned from the most inspired craftsmen of her time—and that was a pretty inspired time. I must hasten to add that these surroundings defy all known rules of arrangement. History's most enchanting connoisseur at home in her boudoir in the midst of her treasures doesn't provide many practical decorating tips, after all.

The rooms that require a lot of care in the arrangement of their furniture are not solitary places; they are rooms in which we entertain others. To dwell on large parties can begin to sound silly. Think, instead, of rooms in which conversation can flourish, whether between two people or among ten, rooms in which visitors feel immediately at home and would rather sit than stand—rooms that really work. I believe that the rooms in which all these things happen are those that are very well arranged. They appear to be comfortable to the eye even before one has experienced the physical comfort.

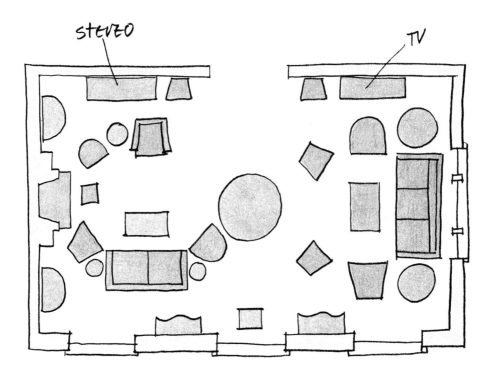

STEREO

TV

I have also observed that in an enormous number of cases all the rooms in a house are perfectly well arranged with the exception of the one that took the most time and money to decorate—the living room. There are several reasons for this failure. One is that in many households the living room is not really a room for living. It just sits there waiting to be looked at but is not used. The visual effect of this disuse is stultifying. Another reason for the lifeless quality of so many living rooms is the owner's desire to please others, to anticipate criticism instead of decorating the room with the same personal point of view that is applied to bedrooms and to more private studies and libraries. More often than not the resulting room is arranged in a stiff stage-set fashion.

A fresh look at the furniture plan would be a good idea for an awful lot of rooms. Here, then, is a little syllogism with which to approach the problem: All rooms look their best if they are used by the people they belong to. Unless a room is arranged in a way that allows it to function comfortably, it will never be used. Therefore, no room will look its best until it is comfortably arranged.

The first thing to do is to be realistic about what you are actually going to do in this living room. If you plan it around dinner parties, then for pete's sake have a lot of dinner parties and make the room suit your favorite kind. A friend and rather scathing social critic once said to me that the reason Madam

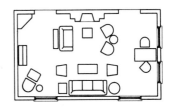

In this living room plan the fireplace is on the long wall, which usually forces us to concentrate the furniture in the middle of the room and gives us the problem of small leftover spaces to be planned for. Here one such space is for reading alone, the other for intimate conversations.

X's dinner parties end so early is that her dining room seats twenty-four and her drawing room seats twelve. As a result, half the guests have to go home after dinner for want of a place to sit, and the other half follow out of the herd instinct. It's no joke.

A big drawing room can seat a lot of people (if that's necessary), but there are a few simple things to remember. You have to have a good many chairs, several of them must be easily moved, and the furniture groupings have to be able to contract and expand as the need arises. It goes without saying that for two dozen guests there must be at least three areas to sit in. It is important that all this furniture be of varying weight and scale. Large and small sofas, large chairs, medium-size chairs, and small chairs. Don't be afraid of stools and benches. And don't listen to that old saw about how three people never sit on a sofa. Beauty or power (or a combination of the two) will load a big comfortable sofa with ardent occupants in a minute. Some of the chair seats should be firm and a little higher than the average reading chair. Lots of people are uncomfortable in low, squushy chairs, and some people fall asleep in them after a big dinner.

So much for the dinner-party room. The best rooms in the world are those that provide us with much more than a place to put guests after a fancy meal. The phenomenal popularity of the English style is the easygoing everyday way the English live in their beautiful sitting rooms—not the way they use their most formal drawing rooms. What could be more normal than having a room in which you can read, listen to music, watch television, and, since it is probably where you like to *be* more than any other place, entertain a few close friends. Start with either the focal point or the primary function, and work from there. The best place for the reading-conversation area is around the fireplace, if there is one. If it is at all possible, it is nice not to wreck the cozy, enclosed feeling of this hearthside arrangement by poking the television right into the middle of it. If, on the other hand, there is no fireplace, then the focal point of the room can be some good-looking (expensive, alas) cabinet work that hides the TV.

The larger view of comfort involves more than the right chair or lighting fixture.

Insufficient light is aggravating, but don't forget that too much light is nearly as bad. Surely every chair doesn't require a reading light, so why not settle on a few places that are terrific for reading and be sure that they are lit in the appropriate way. There is nothing too complicated about dimming the lights when you want a more seductive atmosphere. Most good lamps have more than one bulb in them anyway. I often put one bright white bulb and one lower-wattage pink bulb in lamps that allow it, which enables me to have three varieties of light from a single lamp.

A good reading chair needs a fairly generous table next to it. A second, lower table adds to the comfort; it is the place for a book, a pair of glasses, a drink, an ashtray—whatever. Low tables (I mean about 22 to 25 inches high) are an easier reach when you are relaxing. They are also less apt to be surfaces for decorative clutter, for who wants to knock over a precious, fragile object that is gracefully embellishing a tabletop. The reason for all this clutter, which unfortunately is often overdone, is to make a room look lived in; otherwise it looks and is lifeless.

For the comfortable reading chair, it is useful to have a place for your feet if you want to put them up. This stool needn't be a matching ottoman, although that's all right. The footrest also provides an additional seat for the times when the room is crowded. I love coffee tables that are tough enough to put your feet on. As a student, I once had my ankle (not even my foot) resting on the corner of a library table, and the librarian asked me if I did that at home. When I answered in the affirmative, she told me to leave. I still have no use for a desk you can't put your feet on.

A perfectly comfortable place for a reading chair is completely off by itself, outside the main seating group. In rooms where the main seating group is in the middle and there is not enough space at the ends for separate seating arrangements, an isolated big chair and ottoman and a generous table do not look out of place, and if you draw up another chair or two and use the ottoman as well, you have a place for three or four people if necessary. To my eye, this looks a lot more comfortable and is a lot more functional than a tiny loveseat and two dinky chairs in some cramped leftover space.

The location of the focal point, whether it is a fireplace or a big window with a splendid view or something else, has an enormous impact on how much seating you can get into a room. The most common spot for this focus is in the center of one of the long walls. In most instances where such a central focus exists, it is nearly impossible to avoid arranging the lion's share of the furniture around the middle of the room. As a result, the end areas, unless the room is really big, don't have much space left in which to place full-fledged seating arrangements. If, on the other hand, the fireplace is centered on the short wall at the end of the room, you have the opportunity to use equal halves of the room for generous seating groups. In fact, when I am faced with adding a room to an existing house, I almost always place the chimney on the end wall.

It is interesting to remember that the sort of furniture placement that we all take for granted is completely twentieth century in concept. It is only in our time that people think furniture should be placed in such a way that it never has to be arranged again. In previous centuries it was understood that furniture got moved around a great deal.

In the present time, which is like the nineteenth century in some ways, many different styles of architecture and interior decoration are popular. It is fantastic to turn the pages of a current magazine and find eighteenth- and nineteenth-century houses still lived in with correct period furniture, apartments in New York decorated as though the empress of Russia were the client, contemporary houses built in a variety of styles never seen before. To a large extent, however, the people who live all over this spectrum of personal taste require many of the same furnishings and room arrangements in order to be comfortable. A tall man with a bad back and a good book who wants to glance at the news isn't going to be interested in the design properties of a fifteen-foot-long banquette. Whether he is at home in Vail or on Fifth Avenue, the same rules apply to his comfort and convenience.

The important thing to remember is that regardless of the type of decoration that appeals to you at the moment, you do not have to sacrifice comfort for style. It is, happily, the role of architecture and decoration to give pleasure, not pain. The surface embellishments can be anything from anywhere, but the underpinnings of a room, namely the way it is arranged, have to satisfy real people in real situations. I guess being realistic is always a high priority, even in the ephemeral realm of decorating.

ONE FAMILY,
THREE REMODELINGS

After I decorated two apartments for a young couple, they called me to help them with this country house in New York State. It is a charming Federal-style house built early in this century but there was a major problem concerning the rear façade pictured here. The wall to which we added the pedimented doorway and round window had been solid and blank and ugly—originally intended as bed walls. The lower of the bedrooms became a garden room on which we centered a new garden plan.

The telephone rings. "We would like to talk to you about decorating our apartment." What does a decorator think? First, you wish you could see the person and the apartment at the other end of the line, because sometimes a decorator and a client can never achieve rapport in the realm of taste. After that, you wonder whether the caller is interviewing dozens of other decorators and whether she has just had a falling out with her current decorator. In any case, the first phone call is not a point at which you are filled with cheerful anticipation. You usually rely on that very uncertain realm of impressions made by a voice, then consult your calendar and either make or not make an appointment.

Let's forget about the false starts and the misfires because this is about the sort of experience that makes the business of interior decorating worth all the headaches that seem to be part of the job. You *do* know about the headaches: horrible delivery lags, dye lots that are wrong, orders that are lost and never processed, worse still, orders that are incorrectly filled. And this short list does not include one's own mistakes, those self-induced headaches.

The particular clients I want to talk about exemplify the interaction that a decorator prefers in his work, and I am glad to say that there have been numerous examples over the years. This young couple is one for whom I have decorated and remodeled two apartments and one house. "With whom," I should say, rather than "for whom," because after working together all this time we are more of a decorating team than a decorator and his clients.

The apartment I went to see after their first phone call was in a building dating from the period after World War II—modern but with good plaster walls and spaces not dominated by the projecting beams and protruding

It's a wonderful sight for a decorator to see his rooms gain greater quality through the owner's own activity.

columns that later came to ruin so many contemporary apartment rooms. It consisted of a large living room, a dining room, pantry, kitchen, maid's room, three bedrooms, and three baths. Since there were no children, there was plenty of space, and after a very pleasant meeting, it seemed established that we would get busy in the near future and start working together. The first thing to think about, as is usually the case, was the floor plan of the apartment and the question of exactly how many changes involving construction we had to consider. One of the bedrooms could be turned into a small library, and the entrance hall needed reworking, not only to make it more handsome but also to create a large corner in the adjacent living room for a grand piano, which meant moving an opening.

Converting one of the bedrooms to a library was more complicated. It would obviously be the bedroom nearest the living room, and after some discussion, we all agreed that it would be far better, since the bedroom in question actually adjoined the living room, if there were tall double doors leading from one room to the other. That decision led to the raising and widening of the door into the dining room as well. It was suggested by this young woman, whose name is Karen, that it would be nice if there was a change in the floor levels, and why didn't we consider going up a step to the library. Why not indeed! This was the era of platforms and rooms in which everything seemed to be sliced off on the diagonal. Although my own attitude concerning a space is to acknowledge its physical shape, it was a welcome relief to find that rather then being confined to a timid view of dealing with bland rooms, I was going to be able to make some real changes and some real improvements. At first, numerous sketches and renderings were required. It is often the case that a decorator and a client who barely know each other rely to a great extent on this kind of communication.

After several months of work, the doorway had been moved and pairs of highly polished lacquer doors had been hung in the new taller openings. The architectural atmosphere was a great deal less bland than it had originally been. The raised library and the richly lacquered doors contributed to a far more individual architectural effect and went a long way toward eliminating that

cookie-cutter effect common to modern apartments with so little detailing. At the same time the apartment became more formal and therefore a suitable background for the occasional antique piece. On the hall table, for example, stood a handsome seventeenth-century tortoiseshell-and-ivory dwarf cabinet containing beautiful little doors and drawers and compartments. In the dining room, which was painted a soft Venetian red, there hung a Queen Anne mirror with a frame of red-and-gold japanning, the mirror found well after the paint went up.

I noticed with interest and pleasure that, as the months went by, more lovely objects began to appear. Every time I would visit the apartment—and certainly after a job is completed, those visits become less frequent—I would see something just brought back from London or picked up at the Winter Antiques Show or sent up on approval from a shop on Madison Avenue. Part of the fun of working with this couple is the fact that they have an inexhaustible curiosity about the places and things I love myself. If on their way to

Although the furniture in the country house is late 19th century, we made the curtains in a design of the American Federal period, which is closer to the architecture. I always feel that curtains belong more to a house than to the furniture one puts into it.

you can always add moldings and paneling to rooms where they did not exist before.

London they would ask what I thought a good weekend would be and if I would say, for instance, go up to Derbyshire and see Chatsworth, Haddon, Hardwick, Sudbury, and Kedleston, they would invariably return full of news about Derbyshire.

Rather than being finished with decorating, they were just beginning. It is a wonderful sight for a decorator to watch rooms he has been involved with achieve greater depth and quality through the owner's own taste and activity. But there are two other categories of rooms that immediately come to mind. One is a little dull but not disastrous, namely rooms that become petrified and never change. It is sad but I have actually had people tell me they were going to take Polaroids of the tabletops in order to keep things in place. I always say to clear things off instead because the objects will never go back to the same places and that is what keeps a room alive. The other category is even sadder: rooms that are spoiled by new acquisitions that violate the original concept.

The arrival of babies meant that a move would eventually be necessary, and one day, a few years later, I got a call from Karen and Peter asking if I would like to see an apartment that was probably going to become theirs and that needed work done on it. We made a date to meet in the lobby of the proposed new apartment. The minute I heard the address I was filled with eagerness, because the building in question had been designed in the 1920s by my favorite apartment-house architect, Rosario Candela, an Italian-born American who was responsible for the most beautifully planned and detailed apartments in New York as well as one marvelous building I know of in Chicago. The new apartment was not disappointing. It was a duplex with lots of south light. It had exceptionally good woodwork and plaster cornices and fine proportions in general, which is typical of Candela's work. Just as the contemporary architecture of their first apartment influenced the decoration, the neo-Georgian architecture of the new one provided a stylistic basis for this one. Obviously you can add moldings and paneling to rooms where they did not exist before, and you can strip them from rooms where they *do* exist. How much nicer, however, if the basic architecture is already sympathetic to the desired style of interior design.

162

Of course, there were changes, some of them more extensive than others. The kitchen, pantry, and servants' rooms were radically overhauled, and the bathrooms needed attention. Once all that was under way, the job of decorating could begin. The upholstered furniture from their rather modern apartment was re-covered, and the lines of the arms and backs were made softer to correspond to the architecture as well as the increasingly traditional collecting interests of Karen and Peter.

What had begun as a few pieces of blue-and-white Chinese porcelain acquired as accessories in a blue-and-white bedroom had mushroomed into a lovely collection of very good pots and vases and bowls, mostly Kang Hsi, much of it stored away because the collection had long since outgrown the bedroom. All this terrific porcelain was able to play a major part in the decoration of the new living room. Pieces were arranged on the walls on brackets made just for the job from a design of John Fowler's—cream and white to match the glazing of the walls.

The stair hall, upstairs and down, is painted the same soft Venetian red as the former dining room. All the pictures and objects and most of the furniture from the previous apartment seem more beautiful in the new apartment, and that is what one would expect, since, after all, the new apartment is more beautiful itself. Equally important is the personal quality that develops after several years of collecting and acquiring the things that are needed to complete the decoration of a house. Once again, I experienced that cheering sensation of increasing appeal whenever I visited Karen and Peter in their new apartment. Beautiful knife boxes might appear in the dining room. Or perhaps a lovely bucolic English landscape over the library sofa. If the occasional old piece disappeared completely in the wake of a new acquisition, the reply to my inquiries about current whereabouts would always be, "Oh, that will go to a house in the country some day." And then a third episodic message appeared on my desk saying, "Karen and Peter want you to take a look at a house they just bought in the country."

For the third (and I hope not the last) time, we walked through an empty dwelling. This one is an enchanting fifty- or sixty-year-old house—with

In the dining room of the couple's New York City apartment, early George III chairs flank a later Georgian sideboard against walls painted to resemble blocks of marble.

funny wings and sloping slate roofs and a beautiful colonnaded front veranda—reminiscent of a Virginia house but standing, instead, under enormous old New York maple trees at the end of a stupendous maple-lined lane. Because the house is picturesque, with lots of French windows leading out to the lawn, it could be decorated in any of several moods. It could be whimsical and flowery. It could be done in a chaste Colonial farmhouse style. It could have serious antique furniture, for that matter. While we chatted about these possibilities, I was told of a large number of pieces of nineteenth-century Heywood-Wakefield wicker furniture that Karen had been gobbling up during the past year or so and storing away heaven knows where. Then there were some odd-looking but delightful pieces of turn-of-the-century upholstered furniture, one of which is sitting today in the living room of this house still in its old cretonne slipcover, although we had to add a little ruffle along the bottom since it had shrunk somewhere along the way.

The question of which style to decorate in was therefore answered by the mood of the things that already existed and that were just waiting to find a home. The finished living room has a distinctly American turn-of-the-century look with its dark lacy wicker furniture and its fanciful upholstery, all sitting on raffia mats and covered in old-fashioned cotton materials. You can almost picture Mark Twain puffing away on his cigar there with a bank of ferns and fuchsias in the background.

We were able to indulge in exterior decoration as well. The back wing of the house had, in its original configuration, bedrooms upstairs and downstairs, one over the other. The outside walls of these two rooms made up half an octagon, but the center wall, intended for the bed, was totally blank and surprisingly ugly from the outside. Since the lower of these two bedrooms was destined to become a garden room, we opened up the blank wall with yet another pair of French windows, which on the exterior we surrounded with pilasters and a nicely made pediment, copying a design we found in a book on Annapolis houses. (Annapolis houses have wonderful woodwork.) The new garden plan is centered on this recently created doorway, and, as a result, the house has a real honest-to-goodness functioning garden entrance.

I remember when I went up to hang some pictures with Karen and Peter. It is very easy with three people: one to keep track of the hammer and nails, one to keep track of the ruler and pencil, and one to make the holes in the newly papered walls. As usual, there were lots of pleasant surprises. An enormous and completely wonderful service of Staffordshire earthenware had arrived from some auction room or other and had taken over the Welsh dresser in the dining room. On an entirely different decorative wavelength, the little wooden bedside lamp from Peter's childhood nursery had somehow resurfaced and was happily ensconced in their five-year-old son's bedroom. I felt very much at home, and as I hung a set of plates that Karen had found which were decorated with bows and flowers, the bows resembling those on the little girl's bedroom wallpaper, I took great pains to put the nails in a dark part of the pattern of the paper because I thought (hoped) that in a few years I would probably be taking the plates down and hanging posters of Bruce Springsteen or whomever and I wanted to be sure the nail holes from a previous era would go unnoticed. These jobs are never finished, and the future has lots of lovely surprises in store.

Rooms

SMALL ROOMS, BIG ASSETS

Small rooms seem to be thought of as unimpressive at best, and at worst as a distinct inconvenience. Considered mean and insignificant, small rooms, poor things, are frequently mistreated. Their decorative possibilities are ignored, and as a consequence a lot of really good opportunities, not only for decoration but also for practical use, are overlooked. It's a terrible waste. On the other hand, when necessity compels people to deal one way or another with a small room, the chief concern seems to be making it appear larger than it really is. This neurotic fixation is wasteful too, because it leads people to ignore the very properties of a small room which can make it fun, effective, and economical to decorate. Rather than dwell on the disadvantages of small rooms, it is much more interesting to consider their positive aspects.

Coziness and intimacy are the obvious qualities that are actually easier to achieve in a small room than in a large one. Mr. Badger's house was probably a lot more inviting than Toad Hall. It was a lot more convenient too, I'm sure. Provided there is a backup realm of storage space, like closets and cupboards somewhere nearby, the task of working in a small room (painting, potting, cooking, reading, writing) can be infinitely easier than rambling around in a great big space. One or two rooms that permit a degree of pack-rat behavior are a blessed addition to any household. A space that is completely cluttered looks better than a space that is only cluttered in one corner: that corner inevitably becomes an eyesore.

Since packing a lot of furniture into a small room is usually essential for its comfort and convenience, it is worthwhile to mention that a lot of pattern is a great way to counterbalance the effect of so much furniture in a confined space. Several years ago I helped decorate a weekend house in Connecticut for

169

a family whose New York apartment is large and light and calm, with twentieth-century works of art. By contrast, their farmhouse is composed of a small eighteenth-century core with many additions, all equally small in scale. Off the narrow entrance hall with its steep stairway is a minute sitting room with a fireplace and two windows. The organization of the wall space is symmetrical. Two walls have windows, one wall has the fireplace, and the remaining wall has the door leading out to the hall. The room contains a short but deep sofa, a writing table with a comfortable open armchair, one large upholstered chair with a footstool, and two tiny slipper chairs. There are little end tables and a little bookcase. The room is completely filled. The walls are papered in stripes with a flowered border running around the top. The large furniture is in a big-scale chintz, the small furniture in a small pattern. The carpet is patterned, and the curtains, although plain, have a lot of fancy trim on them. There are prints and drawings everywhere. There are books, photographs, firewood, pillows, and newspapers. It is impossible to be in this room and be far from anything— the fire, the views out the windows, or the books and papers that share the space. Yet with all that pattern within the orderly arrangement of the furniture, the atmosphere is cluttered but tidy and very inviting. And, of course, it is an enormously useful room.

The most prevalent category of small rooms is no doubt that of the bedroom. A guest bedroom in the farmhouse of Keith and Chippy Irvine demonstrates many of the advantages and possibilities of smallness. Mr. Irvine's exuberant gift for whimsy is widely known, and when coupled with his notable tendency to avoid stuffiness, it often results in rooms that possess tremendous comfort and spontaneity. In this wonderful bedroom we can readily see another surprising phenomenon found in the decoration of tiny rooms, namely, the effectiveness of a huge piece of furniture in a cramped space. The big canopy bed, painted a shade of red that evokes the delicious illustrations by Carl Larsson of the rooms he created in his Swedish country house at the turn of the century, takes up about half of the room. What it gives in return for its spatial demands, however, more than justifies its overwhelming presence. It is, first of all, wonderful to look at. We must never forget that one of the cardinal rules of decorating is that the better it looks, the better it is. In a little space a huge bed or bookcase or wardrobe or whatever always takes on an architectural quality far more vividly than in a larger room or in a room with more competitive architectural detail. The Irvines' guest room also has a bookcase, a comfortable bedside table, a generous chest of drawers, more than one chair, and pillows galore. The chairs can be sat on, but they can also be used as tables to drop things on or to drape jackets over in a way only straight-backed chairs

allow. Simple, straightforward comfort is frequently a very easy thing, like more chairs. The provisions of this room, arranged the way they are, could keep anybody happy almost without having to leave the bed.

A well-known monument to the beauty of tiny rooms is the so-called Hunting Lodge in Hampshire, which used to belong to the great English decorator John Fowler and is now occupied by Nicholas Haslam, another of the same, who has happily preserved much of the background decoration from Mr. Fowler's time. That this beguiling house owes a lot to its occupants is obvious. It has, however, great character of its own, which the minuteness of its rooms (and they *are* minute) in no way diminishes. Everywhere you look, you see pattern and color, valances and cornices, borders and fringe, floor tiles and quaintly shaped Gothick windows.

All the lovely decorative variety at Hunting Lodge has another significant aspect and that is its comparative modesty in relation to the ever-increasing prices of furniture and decoration. It is not difficult to grasp the fiscal challenges that face a person today doing up a few rooms with fourteen-foot

In a small cottage hideaway built for Queen Victoria and Prince Albert on the grounds of Balmoral Castle, the Prince's dressing room was a delightful place lined with striped cotton and equipped with a fireplace, daybed, slipper chair, and dressing table. On the patterned carpet: a needlepoint hearth rug.

*Mr. Badger's house was probably
a lot more inviting than
Toad Hall.*

ceilings and windows to match. How sad it is to see a room that needs a really big mirror but doesn't have one and a couple of really big pictures but doesn't have them either. Small rooms permit an entirely different scale of decoration to be carried out. In Mr. Fowler's sitting room, there were some full-size upholstered pieces, light George III and Regency armchairs, bits of needlepoint on pillows, carpets, bellpulls, and touches of patterned cotton and chintz. The rigid effect of a set scheme was nowhere to be found. The same is true of the Irvines' guest bedroom.

By contrast, a strict room I adored was the studio apartment on East 61st Street which was Billy Baldwin's last home in New York. It too was small, and painfully typical of the unfortunate boxlike apartments that thousands of New Yorkers have to put up with. Rather than fret over what was wrong with the space architecturally, Billy simply overcame it with a strong scheme made of very dark brown walls, a trademark of his, shades of cream and off-white, and accents of brass and gold combined with dark lacquer, mostly black and blacky brown. The room contained a lot of furniture—a single bed designed to look like a huge boxy sofa, strict squared-off slipper chairs, the famous Cole Porter bookcases, a Korean screen, a large oblong writing table with a cloth to the floor, a classic sofa, and many small tables of every description and every date. The relentless right angles of the furniture placement made a positive feature out of the monotonous angularity of the architecture. Later on, he combined panels of mirror with the dark brown walls in some awkward corners and created delightful illusions of space where there was none. Mirror work in small rooms can be phenomenally effective. Billy's superb study in discipline proved again that it is a lot more important to look good than to look big.

There are many rooms that actually suffer from being too big. I would much rather have a modest-size bedroom and a big dressing-room storage area than the reverse. When planning closets and cupboards for bedroom suites, I always press for a separate room in which to put them rather than have an

entire wall of doors in the bedroom itself, which can never be satisfactory from an aesthetic point of view.

And the enormous spa bathrooms of our day seem foolish to me. Who wants to move around in a room dedicated to bathing which is so large that you feel as if you have to put something on to walk from one side to the other? Huge kitchens can be exhaustingly inefficient too, unless you have a chef and three kitchen maids. Small hallways are a lot easier to decorate than enormous ones. In fact, hallways and corridors are perfect areas to indulge in the forbidden practice of overdecorating, since they are areas of movement rather than of contemplation. I love wallpapers and borders and moldings and pedestals in a hallway, all sorts of mannered pieces of furniture, and decoration that might appear arch in a space you spend hours in.

If you still think small rooms are not your cup of tea, then I will close with a reminder to look again at some of the most ravishing and seductive rooms on earth—the small private apartments built for Louis XV at Versailles. The rooms are tiny and the ceilings are right down on top of your head, yet with their gorgeous paneling and gilding they simply breathe the purpose they were intended for—privacy and comfort without sacrificing luxury or beauty. The intimacy they achieve would not have been possible on a large scale. In their smallness they have a universal appeal that spans centuries.

Sunny and Howard Sloan's farmhouse sitting room is tiny but is furnished with everything a sitting room requires in a scale that makes only one concession to the room's size: The comfortably deep sofa is shorter than usual. Walls are arranged symmetrically; details are in no way skimpy.

LIBRARIES TO LIVE IN

The maddening but interesting thing about clichés is that they always contain a good bit of truth. Take the expression, "Books do furnish a room," which is even one of the titles in Anthony Powell's brilliant group of novels called *A Dance to the Music of Time*. There is no doubt about the accuracy of the observation, although it is repugnant to many people to place books in the category of decorative accessory: "What are these books *doing* here if they are neither read nor cared about?" they ask. For the purpose of our discussion about libraries and bookcases let us presume that books are vital and that everyone either (a) loves having them around or (b) would be better off if they did. And let us presume that we are not talking about books that are bought by the yard.

There are several libraries that I have loved from photographs for many, many years. A few in particular have become all-time favorites and can, I hope, bear being described again. I say *again* because they have been published over and over, but they are still fascinating. One that I hope to see some day is in the little hermitage built for Madame de Pompadour, that most interesting consumer and lady of fashion. For many years The Pompadour, as it is called, was occupied by the late Vicomte and Vicomtesse de Noailles, two people who must be ensconced in the Pantheon of great brains, taste, and style. The library of this perfect eighteenth-century pavilion is a rather small space, almost cubelike because of its great height. The bookcases go straight to the floor, continuing down behind the tables and the backs of the chairs. The books themselves become the surface of the walls, and the background this surface creates is a wonderful foil for the funny combination of furnishings in the room—Régence chairs, Louis XV chairs, Louis XVI chairs, a big Chinese table, and a Neoclassical Aubusson carpet. It is somehow an ideal room, due in no small part to the inviting atmosphere the books create.

Also in France, but a made-up architectural tour de force like so many of his triumphs, is the library at Groussay, Charles de Beistegui's Valhalla of interior decoration near Versailles. It is a two-story room that has been photographed about as many times as the Statue of Liberty. (I am lucky enough to have an original Cecil Beaton photograph of the room with old seersucker slipcovers on the chairs—what a treasure!) Across one end of this huge room is a U-shaped bank of full-height bookcases with a sort of minstrel's gallery at the top, reached by not one but two spiral staircases of the same mahogany as the bookcases themselves. It is a fabulous room in every way, but all the grand pictures and furniture count for nothing compared with the bookcases.

The more I think about it, the more certain I am that book rooms are my favorite rooms of all. The libraries in the fine teens-through-thirties houses of Chicago architect David Adler were superb. The great Walpole scholar Wilmarth Lewis had, in Farmington, Connecticut, a library designed by Delano & Aldrich—that august firm whose unerring taste seemed to permeate everything they did—a library with bookcases coming out at right angles to the walls and stopping several feet from the ceiling, admitting light from high windows. On top of these bookcases stood busts and great big Chinese vases—absolutely marvelous—and for furniture, there were some chintz sofas and some leather chairs. What could be simpler? These, of course, are more or less real rooms in more or less real houses. In addition, and really staggering, are the *great* libraries.

The most beautiful one I have ever seen and maybe my favorite room on earth is the Imperial Court Library in the Hofburg in Vienna. Filling one whole side of the Josefplatz and about the size of Madison Square Garden, this indescribably beautiful space was designed by Johann Bernhard Fischer von Erlach, a gifted eighteenth-century architect who, like James Gibbs, studied under Carlo Fontana in Rome, and who, also like Gibbs, managed to assimilate a kind of Baroque style that was applicable to the other layers of current taste. This resulted in an original and complicated architecture and decoration that never ceases to take one's breath away, and the Imperial Court Library is too beautiful for words. Without straining your patience, let me attempt to list at least the elements that make up this enormous and glorious space. There is a central dome, rising four or five stories above your head. There are flanking spaces with barrel vaults, connected to the rotunda by screens of Corinthian columns. The materials are warm marble and scagliola in shades of deep cream and terra-cotta along with the mahogany, gilt bronze, and gold leaf of the bookcases and the brown morocco and gilt of the bindings. The ceilings are frescoed. But none of this comes close to describing the atmosphere of musty

The more I think about it, the more certain I am that book rooms are my favorite rooms of all.

but almost celestial goldenness, of books integrated into a color scheme completely organized around the color and texture of the bindings themselves. The rich, earthy tonality surpasses any I have ever seen.

    One aspect of many of these very tall libraries that is interesting to note is the presence of high windows above the tops of the bookcases. The shafts of sunlight filtering down into the somewhat gloomy, book-filled lower portion of the spaces are responsible for the marvelous atmosphere of light and shadow common to so many libraries. Our own stupendous public library in New York has reading rooms lit by high east and west windows, creating lovely light both in the morning and in the afternoon.

    To strive to possess a monumental library is not, of course, what I am recommending. If you have a room in which you can build a lot of bookcases, you are very lucky. The design of a wall or more of new bookcases should, I believe, be simply but carefully integrated into the architectural vocabulary of the house you live in. Particular attention must be paid to cornice and base details. If you do not take the bookcases to the ceiling, then a deft approach to proportion becomes essential, since the interval of wall space above the books has to be large enough to put something on—pictures, sculpture, porcelain. The actual bays of shelves should be worked out in some rhythmic program based either on principles of symmetry or as a reflection of the windows, doors, and so forth on the wall opposite. I must also add that the bays of shelves should not be too long, because even the thickest of shelves will warp under

This sort of bookcase is simple, handsome, and useful. Antique examples can be found or new ones can be made, with variations in the base and pilasters, by any competent carpenter. I designed this particular bookcase for our family scrapbooks.

This superb library designed by Delano & Aldrich for Wilmarth Lewis in Farmington, Connecticut, has a tall barrel-vaulted ceiling and lovely provisions for daylight: two tiers of deep-set windows and a floor-to-frieze arched window at the end of the room. At the same time a coziness was created by the bookcase alcoves and by such furnishings as chintz sofas, leather chairs, and old-fashioned wooden window blinds.

the weight of too many books. Thin shelving is a disaster. There are also countless possibilities below the shelves for cabinets with doors. These cabinets can line up with the height of the windowsills, or they can relate to writing-table height—somewhere between 28 and 31 inches high. If this line gets too high, then the whole thing looks clumsy. High-waisted breakfront bookcases are not nearly so highly prized as low-waisted ones. If you need doors above as well, to hide guns or liquor or the dreaded television set, they can be paneled, or covered with grillwork, or they can have glass panes if protection is all that is required. I, by the way, love false bindings when they are subtly made, but lots of people shriek with disapproval when I suggest them. They are not difficult to have made, though, and the deception can be marvelous.

The easiest thing, however, is to put books in freestanding bookcases, which exist in an enormous variety of styles and finishes and which can be placed anywhere you want them. The most familiar sort of all is, I suppose, the mahogany breakfront bookcase with glass doors above and cabinets below. How or why it got lined with silk and turned into a china cupboard I'll never know. If you own one and have it in your dining room filled with porcelain, please forgive me, but they do look better filled with books. Secretary bookcases are both useful and beautiful, too, especially when the writing part is open, displaying lovely inkwells and candlesticks and objects that fit into all the little cubbyholes. In addition, they hold a lot of books. We have one in our living room and it has about 120 books in it, all categorized and easy to locate. The ability to lay your hands on a particular book is sometimes very elusive.

Another classic bookcase style that fits into an incredibly varied number of decorative styles is the Directoire brass-and-steel étagère, a version of which was made famous by Billy Baldwin in the Waldorf Towers apartment of Cole Porter. This wonderfully flexible design can have shelves of polished wood, lacquer, or glass. It can be any size, and if you order one so tall and skinny that it tips, you can always bolt it to the wall.

A large and rather neglected bookcase category, which I have illustrated, ranges in height from 45 to 60 inches. If you can't find an antique example, a cabinetmaker or even a carpenter can make you one. Since it is freestanding, such a piece can have a base closely related to the baseboard molding of the room. But if that is too heavy, it can be more lightly scaled. The corner pilasters can also follow many different design paths: scrolls, fluted columns, blocky columns with complicated bases, Postmodern essays in Neoclassicism—the list is quite long. Recently, I visited Olana, the beautiful Columbia County, New York, house of Frederic Church. In the hall are four lovely little oak bookcases, handsomely detailed by the artist himself with lots of deeply cut moldings. They are filled with books as they should be. On the tops are collections of exotic objects of the sort that fill this most exotic of houses, and that is the beauty of these bookcases. They are simple pieces of furniture that in addition to holding books support a wide variety of objects, photographs, or small works of art. They also provide a place for lamps, and regardless of what you put on them, those things will be at a height that makes them easy to look at, well above the often monotonous line of normal table heights. But the main thing is to get bookcases into your life and to fill your house with the most reliable companions imaginable.

INVITING GUEST ROOMS

Before I encountered the seductive luxuries of Porthault linens and the coffee tray brought by the maid who comes to open the shutters, my favorite guest room in the world was my Aunt Edith's sleeping porch in northern Indiana with its six iron bedsteads and its ancient bedding (freezing cold when you got in but terribly comfortable) and its aroma of pine trees coming through the screens. There was a distant view of a lake beyond, and to a landlocked Middle Westerner that lake held all the exciting promise of the Mediterranean Sea. Those August weekends of forty years ago have provided me with perfect summer memories (with the exception of a particularly awful incident involving a purple crayon I applied to a newly slipcovered sofa)—picnics around fires on the beach, corn on the cob at least once a day, and staying up till all hours on hot nights.

Central to all this nostalgia, however, is the house and how I loved staying in it. The total effect of my aunt's welcoming disposition was marvelous to me. This intangible, enormously important aspect of hospitality seems to be inborn. People who are temperamentally ill-suited to receiving overnight guests can inflict untold miseries on their hapless victims, and we all learn to avoid invitations to spend a night or two in houses where the atmosphere resembles a Dickensian orphanage. But oh, the fun of arriving at a house and feeling the immediate spark which tells you that you are going to have a good time and you are going to be comfortable. Let's forget about trying to analyze that spirit of playful generosity so vital to the emanation of real hospitality. It would be too difficult and abstract. Let us dwell, instead, on the material side of things, which after all reflects something of the personalities of the hosts and hostesses we all love and adore.

Guest rooms are different from all other decorating efforts because while they inevitably reflect the taste of their owners, they are created for others to use. Therefore you cannot say about your guest room, "I like it, so the hell with it." Guest rooms must give instant pleasure to many people. There are guest rooms in all sizes and colors, grand or modest, old-fashioned or modern. Whatever they are, they should be welcoming. It should be a pleasure for guests to close the door and make themselves feel temporarily at home.

Consider grand guest rooms. One thing they should not be is intimidating. Grandeur should be fun. For years, before the house was sold, we used to stay near Oxford with friends who had a variety of guest rooms ranging from small and cluttered to large and airy, the latter used primarily in the summer. The best one of all was in the main part of the house directly at the top of a flight of broad stairs. It is always pleasant when the guest room is easy to reach and doesn't involve what feels like an invasion of the most private precincts of the house. This heavenly room was tall and rather stately, to use that corny word, with handsome plain paneling painted shades of cream color and the moldings carefully picked out in white. The rest of the colors were warm and rosy—creamy peach, reds, and aubergine. The main event of the room was an enormous canopy bed with a domed top, which was marvelous to look at from both outside and inside. It was beautiful and fun at the same time. The comfort of this room reached its peak in the bathrooms and dressing rooms—plural—one for the woman and one for the man. I've seen a number of guesthouses and guest suites with little sitting rooms that do not seem to be heavily used, but double dressing rooms and baths are very useful and incredibly luxurious.

Another guest room memorable for its terrific glamour was in the little house in the south of France called Le Clos Fiorentina, where Rory Cameron lived first in the forties when he was remodeling La Fiorentina, that legendary Palladian house overlooking the Mediterranean, returning to it later in the seventies after the big house had been sold.

Le Clos was a simple house filled with the fascinating variety of beautiful things that characterized all of Rory Cameron's houses. A great deal of the furniture had found its way there after having been in more imposing surroundings, and the guest room, looking out across a vine-covered terrace to a view of the sea, was furnished with a suite of elaborate mirrored furniture made in Paris in the twenties. There were bedside tables, a dressing table, and even a semainier totally covered in beveled mirror. The bed was draped in a sheer gauzy material and the floor was covered in the very fine straw matting sewn together with linen threads that is made in the south of France and is the prettiest summer floor possible. It is also expensive and doesn't last very long, so it is not tops on the list of helpful hints for thrifty homemakers. The movie-star quality of this room was perfectly suitable to the way the house was run and to its location on one of the most chic stretches of seashore on earth. It was unpretentious and just happened to have a lot of witty furniture used in a subtle tongue-in-cheek way.

If you think of your guest room as part of the whole process of entertaining your guests, then why not be a little whimsical? A house I adore to visit has a stupendous guest room that was, before a siege of remodeling a few years ago, the master bedroom. It is elliptical and of all the neglected architectural forms of the past, nothing is lovelier than an oval room.

As you approach the room down its little passageway, the first thing you see is an old fireplace, which in the wintertime always has a fire flickering away in it. The next big treat in store is the bed itself, a chinoiserie four-poster extravaganza with a pagoda top. When you are in this great bed, you look out of the big French windows to a view of lawn, elm trees (the loveliest of all endangered species of anything, as far as I'm concerned), and acres and acres of

Oh, the fun of arriving at a house and feeling the spark that tells you that you are going to have a good time.

This little guest room in
Joanne and Alfred Stern's country
house is lined with lavender-and-
white wallpaper. The old iron beds,
marble-top washstand, and white
batiste curtains are typical
of American country rooms a
century ago.

rolling New York farmland. It has always occurred to me, while staying in these perfect surroundings, that when remodeling, it makes great sense to convert the master bedroom into a really good guest room and then start all over with a new master suite.

Summer-house guest rooms, rooms that often have little or no cold weather use, are loaded with opportunities for easy and even economical decorating. (I sometimes wonder if there are any easy and economical areas of interior decoration left in the world.) A hodgepodge of leftover furniture can be easily and simply painted—either a color or white—and made to go together in an offhand way that is very appealing.

I remember a favorite example in a Southampton house that was furnished with a lot of typical bedroom furniture all of which had been painted a soft medium tone of green and then pinstriped in white. Like the walls, the floor was painted white, and was covered with a cotton rug, which is the most comfortable thing of all under bare feet. Watercolors and prints with pale mats and painted frames hung all around the room, and everything—curtains, dust ruffles, and furniture—was made up in the same pink-and-green printed cotton. Painting all the furniture to match and using a single material had the effect of unifying a lot of disparate, maybe even cast-off, stuff. The result was charming and comfortable because nothing was missing. By that, I mean there was a place for everything you might travel with, and all the utilitarian furniture without which a guest room can be irksome was there.

The most indispensable piece of furniture that is frequently omitted from guest rooms is a writing table. Not to be able to sit down and do a little desk work is maddening. It is exactly the sort of work you cannot do in a room where other people are sitting, nor do you want to use someone else's desk. In a guest room, however, what is nicer than a table that invites you to sit down, even open the drawers in search of a piece of paper or a pencil, and, as the country saying goes, make yourself at home? This important piece of furniture is also the place where the host can put the books selected for the weekend visitor if the room is too small for a bookcase, and where a bowl of fruit and some writing implements can be added.

My favorite book story involves a famous European chatelaine who had rented her house to an equally famous American. The owner of the house called a friend of mine in London frantically asking whether or not her imminent tenant's maid was French. What difference does it make, asked my friend, whereupon this legendary paragon of housekeeping replied, "I'm selecting the books for the maid's room."

Entertaining weekend guests offers myriad ways to pamper your friends. The bathroom with its full-length mirror, its outlet for curlers and hair dryers, and its well-stocked medicine cabinet seems perfectly obvious. It can be a huge relief to find a sewing kit or a clothes steamer when emergencies arise. A welcoming kitchen with a generously stocked refrigerator is appreciated, too, provided you don't slip up and eat the next day's lunch, as I once did to my horror. (Imagine the horror of my hostess!) My wife's pet peeve is not being able to sleep on the pillow that is provided, so she travels with her own. Who invented foam rubber pillows anyway? Guest beds should be equipped with one soft, one firm, and one baby pillow for every person who is supposed to sleep in that bed.

The pivotal quality that makes any house a delight to visit is the spirit of the people who live there. In the absence of a positive love of housekeeping and decorating, no house will ever be charming or attractive, and without enjoying the company of overnight guests, one probably will never achieve a very satisfying guest room. (Inspecting guest rooms can, in fact, provide some rather wicked insights into the personalities of the owners.) Those who doubt their genuine love of their fellow man should perhaps use that spare room for luggage and Christmas wrappings.

THE INTEGRITY
OF THE DINING ROOM

In a house in Texas the dining room, which is used only at night, was made dramatically dark. I created paneled walls and filled the panels with mirrored glass to reflect the guests and the table settings, such as this one including blanc de chine, silver gilt, and orchids. Some elements are dark green (walls, curtains, table skirt); others are black (horsehair chair seats, needlepoint carpet's background).

More than any other room in the house, the dining room is a place for old traditions, a scene of ritual use where we can indulge in memories of the way our parents and grandparents did things in days gone by. We can put to use objects we have inherited from previous generations without their seeming like irrelevant artifacts. Many otherwise modern people when using their dining rooms actually enjoy returning to the vanished world of manners commonly thought to have been more gentle and refined than our own.

Thinking back to thirty or forty years ago, I seem to remember that dining rooms weren't faring so well. Ranch-house architecture gave birth to floor plans that didn't even *have* dining rooms half the time. For apartment dwellers whose space was limited, decorators were advocating turning the dining room into a library with a round table and four chairs tucked into the corner. Maybe it had something to do with the new phenomenon of the TV tray. Many of these hybrid rooms still exist, but the genuine dining room is once again a healthy species, and if all the interest in cooking and flower arranging and collecting antiques is as prevalent as I think it is, then dining rooms will be more used and more useful as time goes on.

Most family festivities are observed around the dining table. When I think about the dining rooms in my childhood and in the considerably more recent past, the memories of what took place in those rooms instantly come to mind. I remember the dining room in the house where I spent the first twenty-four years of my life more vividly than any other room there. My parents were fond of antiques, and from the time my sister and I were conscious of our surroundings we knew that the old furniture was somehow better than the rest. The dining room in our house was full of antiques. The chairs were prettier

The furnishings in our Manhattan dining room (another detail shown on page 17) span several centuries: 17th- century engravings, 18th-century Irish console table, 19th-century Gothic Revival chairs, 20th-century patterned carpet.

than the maple ones we sat on in the breakfast room. They also required our being careful (one of them was always out being repaired). Everything about the dining room was special, and we had to be on our best behavior whenever we were allowed in that superior world. But that didn't bother us. We were always dying to eat there; and now, forty years later, we both love using the things that come from that room, things that are full of wonderful memories. There is one particular appliquéd organdy tablecloth my mother made about fifty years ago that my sister, Rachel, Mother, and I still pass back and forth and it always reminds me of the first daffodils (this cloth was usually used at Easter) that decorated the table. As I recall the plates and the silver we used in the dining room (never in the maple world of the breakfast room), it occurs to me that the real treasures that most families keep and revere are from the dining room. The Cellini saltcellar did not sit on the entrance hall table of Francis I, after all.

One of my favorite dining rooms is in a Manhattan apartment that was decorated by Billy Baldwin over twenty-five years ago. For the past seventeen years, I have helped the fastidious owner preserve it in one way or another. The

I remember the dining room of the house where I grew up more vividly than any other room there.

other rooms have gradually been redecorated, but the dining room stays the same. It contains the classic ingredients for a successful room that can perform either in a formal or informal way. The walls are papered in a softly printed large-scale pattern of geometric fretwork in café au lait on cream. The carpet was originally the familiar beige and off-white Maltese cross pattern laid wall to wall. I had to replace it a couple of years ago, but did not upset the ecology of the room. The same thing happened with the off-white curtains when they were redone. We opted for a similar material, made in a similar way.

This conservative, preservationist point of view has been, over the years, the result of our wanting to keep the background in place for a beloved collection of marvelous furniture. There is a huge, faded mahogany demilune sideboard, a mirror-polished pedestal table, also mahogany, that seats six or expands for sixteen, and an Indian ivory-framed mirror with eighteenth-century mercury glass panels set in squares, each panel separated by ivory mullions like a window. If this room sounds conventional, it is not. The chandelier is French, and the chairs are contemporary versions of Hepplewhite with white crackle lacquer frames that have an almost Art Deco look. The pictures range from a Japanese screen to a Vuillard. Because the room is so pale, it's divine at lunch time, with the East River gliding by, yet in candlelight it becomes softly traditional and formal. With all its chic glamour, it is still firmly planted in the time-honored past.

Searching for a way to blend modern stylishness with a fundamentally traditional look frequently leads to exciting and wonderfully original rooms. A famous New York example belongs to Nan and Tommy Kempner and has been for thirty years the setting for lunches and dinners of every description—all of them terrific. With walls covered in antique painted Chinese silk, you'd think it would be staid and old-fashioned. On the other hand, its collection of Chinese glazed earthenware figures mounted on contemporary brackets and lit from recessed ceiling lights might give you the impression that it's dramatically modern. Yet there is no confusion here. The room is simply a fabulous combination of the new and the old. The table and chairs are eighteenth-century English, as is the plain but beautiful George I chandelier, which burns real candles. On the floor there is a Victorian needlepoint carpet. Instead of curtains, solid paneled shutters hang at the windows, wood-grained to match the brackets on the walls. Behind this setting for some of the best parties I know of is the collaboration between Mrs. Kempner and the late Michael Taylor. The decorator's hand is evident everywhere in an apartment that brilliantly combines a love of decorating and collecting with a recognition of the essential need for comfort.

Most important to the Kempners are the food and the guests, the real point of the room, after all. Here is where the talent of the host and hostess lies. We should all remember that dining rooms are really stage sets. The decorating job isn't finished until there is a meal on the table and the people on hand to bring the whole thing to life. In order for a dining room to have any heartbeat at all, it has to be used. How often you use it and the variety of the table settings and menus you are capable of producing determines the true success of the room.

The prevailing atmosphere can be one of opulence or of restraint, or it can be a subtle combination. Bill Blass's dining rooms both in New York and in Connecticut are spare and disciplined in their decoration, clearly revealing the perfect eye of their owner. The one in town is strongly architectural and Neoclassical, with columns and busts and pediments. Its sumptuous urbanity is achieved by the use of ravishing white flowers and precious antique accessories—huge decanters in lacquered coasters, tortoiseshell and ivory boxes, and superb eighteenth-century candlesticks, not to mention beautiful plates and silver, which are always old and rare.

In Connecticut, his dining room is dominated by a vast rustic fireplace and a pair of high-back George II hall benches that flank the table and seat the guests. A pair of demilune tables, painted in a faux bois finish, and a severe side table can be used for serving or to support the plants and flowers that decorate this otherwise restrained room. When the fire is burning and the candles are lit

My sister, Rachel, and her husband live in an 1880s shingled house in Illinois where their dining room retains its original fireplace and moldings. Chairs at the round table—mahogany pieces found in London—are from the middle of the 19th century. The tole chandelier was originally a gas fixture.

We should all remember that dining rooms are really stage sets.

and there is a big chicken pie bubbling away on the sideboard, the austere mood dissolves into an atmosphere of warm hospitality and unexpected visual delight.

Although it is not quite as easy to turn an elaborately decorated dining room into a setting for simple meals as it is to do the reverse, it can be done. I remember a marvelous Sunday buffet supper outside London in a grand dining room more accustomed to formal meals. This high-ceilinged room with an enormous glass chandelier and tall windows swagged and festooned with silk damask is the epitome of Georgian refinement and scale. In addition to a very big Chippendale pier mirror between the windows, a Gainsborough and a Van Dyke portrait hang on the walls. The fireplace is opposite the windows. Heroic mahogany sideboards stand on the flanking walls.

For most of us, this does not sound like the right room for a buffet, but it was. On each sideboard the hostess had set out identical platters of cold ham and chicken, French and Italian sausages, eggs in mayonnaise, cold artichokes and asparagus, and the inevitable smoked salmon. There were boards of various cheeses and baskets of toast and crackers. At the end of each sideboard stood a big bowl of Russian salad, one of my favorite cold dishes, and in the center tall silver epergnes were filled with fruit. The display was deliciously luxurious without being grotesque because the menu was so refreshing and light. One amusing aspect of this sort of meal in a house full of beautiful silver and vermeil was the way the service was laid out on either side of our plates: There were four or five sizes and shapes of everything, to be used or not, depending on what we chose from the sideboards.

There is a whole category of small, darkly rich dining rooms that should be mentioned. Better for dinner than for breakfast and lunch, these rooms can sparkle and vibrate with the colors of flowers and candlelight. For years Lee Radziwill Ross had an enchanting square dining room on Fifth Avenue with rosy red walls that were an ideal background for every flower color—whether real flowers or those painted on porcelain. All the furniture was Regency, lavishly ornamented with gilded dolphins and griffons. There were cabinets and consoles that combined black-and-gold chinoiserie panels with painted bamboo pilasters and palm trees. The carpet was a delicate pale Bessarabian that for some reason was not destroyed by chair legs going back and forth, but that is part of the mysterious enchantment that hovers over all the houses of this extraordinary woman.

Several years ago I redecorated a small dining room in a house where breakfast and lunch are usually served on a sunny porch overlooking the garden. The dining room, therefore, could be decorated as a nighttime environment. Because it was small, I added moldings to form panels all around the room and filled each panel with mirrored glass. We painted the walls dark green and curtained the window, which I widened and lowered to the floor, with matching silk taffeta. The round table was skirted in green damask and surrounded by Venetian chairs painted in green and gold (very old and worn) and covered in black horsehair. Over it hung a Louis XV chandelier. For the side walls we found a pair of white marble Italian console tables that stand out dazzlingly against the dark green and mirror of the walls. A collection of gilt-bronze candlesticks and white porcelain figures with bronze mounts decorates the table and the consoles. Underneath all this lies a needlepoint carpet with a black background and sprays of garden flowers. Granted this is no place for peanut butter and jelly, but any candlelight dinner with virtually any selection of flowers looks spectacular in these glittering surroundings. And the element of intimacy always adds to the delight of a dinner party.

Whether your tastes lead you in the direction of polished mahogany, giltwood, bleached pine, or even glass and steel, you should think twice before you turn your dining room into something else. No other room in the house allows you to exercise your creative instincts as often and with such variety as the dining room does.

STRUCTURE AND DECORATION
IN BATHROOMS

This bathroom in a 19th-century house on Long Island was completely remodeled and redecorated starting with the incorporation of two closets to enlarge the space. We were able to give the new room its architectural quality by planning it symmetrically and taking pains with the woodwork and cabinetwork. The arches and Gothic details were inspired by the old chintz that we used on the walls.

O f all the remodeling and redecorating projects undertaken in one's life, none is more difficult and complicated than working on a bathroom. Everything about the topic is numbing: the design problems, the spatial requirements, the utilitarian demands, the enormous expense, and the ridiculous amount of time all this punishment takes. To begin with, there is the long list of tradesmen required to do a proper job (not including the two architects and four decorators you have no doubt interviewed): the carpenter-builder, the plumber, the tile man or marble man or both, the floor man, the mirror man, the electrician, the painter, and perhaps the paperhanger as well. How many have I left out?

It is possible and often preferable to do a superficial job, working with the good points that already exist. Often, however, there just aren't enough good points. Their absence is the real reason for plunging into the abyss of renovating in the first place. But you should be sure of what you are doing before you begin tearing up floors and walls and exposing all the wires and pipes. This surgery takes a lot of thinking, looking, and planning. I don't want to go into the utilitarian aspects of bathrooms here though; instead I would like to bring up a few architectural and decorative issues.

Bathrooms allow us to be more extreme in style than we might want to be in the rest of the house. In many otherwise timid or conservative establishments I have seen baths where overindulgent decorating doesn't seem to bother a soul. What would look vulgar in any other room looks great in the private precincts of the bath. In one wonderful Westbury, Long Island, house built in the Georgian style about sixty years ago, everything is refined and traditional—old carpets and good English furniture in rooms with simple curtains and subdued colors. But in the master bath the Art Deco period leaps out at you with lacquered walls, a marble floor, and stainless-steel scallop shells applied to the cornice. The mirrors are bordered with stainless steel, and the sink stands on huge Lucite legs. The toilet is hidden by a steel-and-lacquer folding screen. It is clearly the one place where a longing for extravagant luxury had won out over the stricter viewpoint prevailing elsewhere.

And so it is with rich bathrooms. They provide a place for private pampering, for a sybaritic mood that might otherwise be frowned upon. Hidden from the scrutiny of others, these rooms are secret havens of self-absorption. Perhaps this indulgent attitude used to be confined to the rich or the racy, but with the introduction of steam baths, Jacuzzis, hot tubs, and the like, the days of self-denial are now in the past. (Let's not even discuss the exigencies of installing tubs that are big enough for more than one person—the structural underpinnings for the weight, the excessive space consumed.)

In the twenties, when the plumbing industry was new, bathrooms were often clinically modern with a stingy sense of confinement. To be sure, not all modern bathrooms are meager; I have seen some wonderful ones—remarkable tours de force of marble and steel with perfectly executed plasterwork and terribly sophisticated custom lighting—but they are impossible to pull off in most buildings, and watered-down attempts are disappointing and banal. The ideal to me is a room of a certain age with a little fireplace and old paneled doors behind which are tucked storage spaces and plumbing fixtures. This sort of room is not often available, yet the same approach with regard to cabinetwork, coziness, visual charm, and comfort can be applied to the planning of a new bathroom.

Several years ago I remodeled an old farmhouse on Long Island for a couple whose taste for collecting and decorating gives their houses great style and charm. We enlarged one of the bathrooms by adding the space of two adjoining closets to come up with a room, albeit a small one, that had some architectural possibilities. Since it was on a corner of the house, it could have two windows instead of the existing one, each facing a different view of the garden. With a window on each outside wall, we were able to place the tub under one of them (projecting into the room rather than flat against the wall) and the sink under the other. In the corners flanking the tub we built two little arched pavilions with mirrored niches inside. In one niche we put the toilet, in the other the shower.

It is possible and often preferable to do a superficial job, working with the good points that already exist.

For a little bathroom in our Long Island house I converted a Regency mahogany shaving stand in the form of an Ionic column into a sink with a nickle-plated basin and a green marble top.

We covered the walls with an old chintz, printed in a pattern of Gothic arches and flowers, that had come from the walls of a beautiful room in an apartment decorated years before by Robert Denning and Vincent Fourcade. (When a client of mine had bought the apartment, I retrieved the old chintz and kept it in a box under my desk for ages, waiting for the perfect place to put it.) Using the chintz as inspiration, we glazed the new windows with mullions shaped into Gothic points. The molding and paneled cabinetwork were painted and dragged in deep cream and white, and all the fittings were finished in polished brass. Old brass light fixtures were fairly easy to locate, as well as an old brass soap rack for the tub. The marble man was able to find a few

197

Christian Dior's bathroom in his chateau is a dream of imperial luxury come true, from the hammered silver urns that hold the hot water to the old marble tub.

pieces of a lovely old tan marble called Hautville, which we used in the shower stall, on the sink top, and around the tub. Combined with the other elements, the marble contributed the look of something built years ago. The wall space sacrificed for the windows is more than made up for by wonderful light and beautiful views. More often than not, windows are more important than wall space in bathrooms. It is amazing to think of all the baths that have no windows at all!

Another ideal bathroom design category is the Ritz Hotel style, based on the baths of the famous luxury hotel chain founded in 1898. The old bathrooms in the London Ritz, before they were yanked out and modernized, were sublime. The sinks and the huge tubs (they had to be smashed in two to get them out of the building) were in one area, the toilets in another, and there was always room for a painted dressing table, chair, and small chest of drawers.

what would look vulgar in any other room looks great in the private precincts of the bath.

The Paris Ritz has been more or less continuously renovated, but its bathrooms have never had a bad remodeling. Their woodwork and cabinetry show the stamp of the true Ritz style. It is nearly always a restrained Edwardian version of the Louis XVI period. César Ritz was very smart, after all, and he knew that the florid C-scrolls of Louis XV might look a little vulgar in the bathroom. Along with late eighteenth-century Classicism, symmetry is always a strong element of the design of these gorgeous baths, with paneling and mirrorwork continuing the balanced placement of all the beautifully executed necessities. Crisp pilasters organize the schemes, providing framing for mirrors, niches, and cabinets.

In one of Ogden Codman's turn-of-the-century baths at The Breakers in Newport, where the wall moldings and the architectural trim of the room evoke the calm of ancient Rome as well as eighteenth-century France, the tub is detailed to look like a modern-day version of a sarcophagus, its sides decorated with the familiar strigil pattern. I fully realize that these glamorous old bathrooms depended for their beauty and luxury on a fairly large square footage. There is a contemporary trend, in this era of "spa" bathrooms, toward allotting vast spaces for the principal bathrooms of the house. Where such space exists, I recommend a fresh study of the bathrooms of sixty or ninety years past.

Not many years ago I was asked to redesign parts of a house that had been through several previous remodelings. High on the list of priorities was an elaborate renovation of the dressing room and bath off the master bedroom. As usual, not enough space existed to satisfy the owners, but the problem was solved in a funny way. On one of my visits to the house, I found that the entire master bedroom wing (a product of a particularly poor building period) had disappeared. The great rubble-filled hole in the ground where the wing had

Another ideal design category is the Ritz Hotel style.

stood was the result, I was gleefully told, of dry rot. An entirely new bedroom would have to be drawn up, along with the necessary dressing rooms and baths—now to be plural.

What we arrived at was an up-to-date version of that well-tested formula which begins with an English-looking bathroom for the man of the house, with handsome paneled cabinets, William Morris wallpaper, and a large stall shower rather than a tub. For his wife we built a large square bathroom with four symmetrical elevations and all of the decorative details that recall the spirit of the Ritz Hotels, Ogden Codman, and Elsie de Wolfe, more or less in that chronological order. One wall of this room is devoted to the tub with its marble surround and pilasters. Another wall at a right angle to the tub is for the sink cabinet and dressing table with more pilasters. The pilasters serve a triple function: They separate the panels of mirror, they contain the sockets for the wall-mounted lights, and they are beautiful. The third wall has a French window opening onto a tiny walled patio, and the fourth has a pair of doors, one to the next room and one to the toilet and bidet. The floor is made of white marble squares with small black marble inserts at the corners. There is room for a couple of small tiered tables and a pair of Louis XVI slipper chairs. All the complexities of contemporary plumbing and electrical work are submerged in the tranquility of a well-ordered plan based on traditional principles of architecture and decoration.

Often it is unnecessary to make any serious changes in a bathroom—all it needs is decorating. My own bathroom in Manhattan, for example, still has its original wall and floor tiles from the 1930s as well as its original plumbing fixtures. I papered the walls and ceiling in my favorite Gothic Revival wallpaper designed by Pugin for the Houses of Parliament in the second quarter of the nineteenth century. Since the window is full size and I did not want curtains to get in the way, I kept the existing wood and grillwork shutters that had been installed in the 1950s. I had the wood painted and woodgrained in a faux mahogany finish along with the rest of the trim. The material used to back the shutter grillwork and to make the sink skirt is an old chintz. The wallpaper, paintwork, and chintz have lasted for eighteen years. The floor has been covered with a succession of patterned wool carpets or rush matting.

In addition to the fixtures, this only slightly larger than average bathroom contains a Regency cabinet in the shape of an oversized pedestal, a cupboard with ten drawers and two doors, a hall chair, and a towel trestle—all in mahogany. The walls are covered with brackets and shelves, watercolors and photographs. It is a room full of memorabilia as well as a large range of necessities, from socks and handkerchiefs to extra tubes of toothpaste and bars of bath soap. I know where everything is; it is one of the few places where I vie with no one for control. Tearing it all up eighteen years ago would not have improved a thing.

The design principles of the past that I so often rely on can be just as helpful in the design of contemporary-looking bathrooms as they are in those with a traditional viewpoint. A friend of mine recently had a brilliant bathroom designed by Robert Bray and Michael Schaible. On the one hand it seems to have grown out of the Bauhaus family tree, but on the other hand it conveys a mood of balanced solidity and richness more evocative of old-fashioned bathrooms. All of the hardware is overscaled and finished in mirrored chrome. The floor, tub surround, and sink counter are made of thick gray granite immaculately seamed and finished. The walls are stark white, and the mirrorwork, although sleek and minimalist in its design, is so carefully detailed that it creates an atmosphere of sparkling luxury equal to the effect of a dozen rock crystal sconces.

If I were a psychiatrist, I think I would like to inspect my patients' bathrooms before investigating any other area of their lives. Your own bathroom should reflect you. Why should anyone else have any say about it? Along with your bedroom, the bathroom is the room you use most regularly. If you are lucky enough to have a bathroom all your own, it should be treated as your refuge from the world.

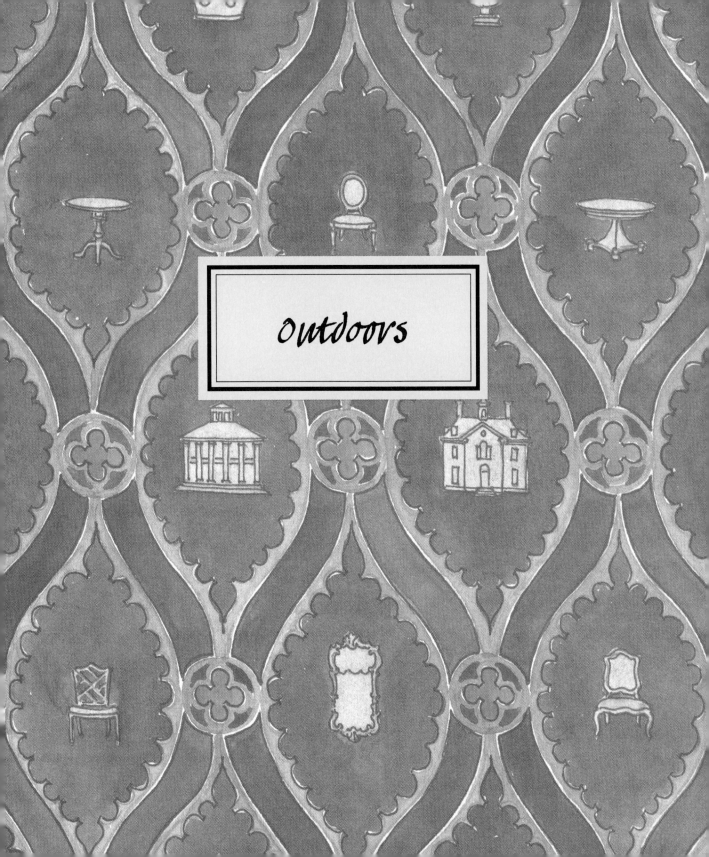

Outdoors

THE ALL-AMERICAN PORCH

Overlooking a salt pond on eastern Long Island, the Italianate porch of Kenneth and Evelyn Lipper's 1870 clapboard house is furnished with pots of geraniums and twenties wicker furniture painted shutter green with cushions covered in a wide-striped canvas. The railing had been removed years ago so that the pond and the old maples could be seen.

In summer I think of porches: the nostalgic, varied, old-fashioned, enormously comfortable and sometimes terribly stylish porches of American houses, outfitted for a long, hot season. The porch with its rocking chairs, old sofas, wicker, gliders and swings, its iced tea and palm-leaf fans, its hanging plants dripping on painted planks—this porch is, in fact, an American phenomenon. The idea of a warm-weather outdoor retreat is so exotic to the English mind that it practically doesn't exist in English houses. What we call a porch, the English call a veranda, a word taken from the Hindi and suggesting the intense heat of India. One of the pleasantest porchlike places ever seen in Britain was not a porch at all. It was Cecil Beaton's winter garden, which was half glassed-in roofed gallery, half greenhouse, with Gothick mullions at the windows, a profusion of basket furniture, blue-and-white Chinese porcelain pots and garden seats, and masses of flowers.

To some architectural historians the American porch as a summer living space has Southern antecedents. Practically every example of Southern American domestic architecture, whether Palladian, Greek Revival, or French or Spanish Colonial in its origin, includes in a major frontal way a porch, call it what you will. This tradition seems to have lodged itself in the mind of the American builder just as firmly as that of green shutters. The marvel of the climate in the United States is that even in Minnesota, Michigan, and Maine, not to mention the other northern latitudes where winters are so unforgiving, the summer months are regularly and dependably hot and sunny. Consequently, the architecture of American houses, whether built for year-round use or for summers, has come to include an encyclopedic variety of porches. Moreover, the porch as a summer living room exists as a happy appendage to the grandest of houses whatever their style.

The front porch tradition has lodged itself in the mind of the American builder as firmly as that of green shutters.

A porch that is very familiar to many people is the west porch of Westbury House on Long Island, New York, which is open to the public. This great Phipps house was built in the first decade of this century. The porch is the perfect marriage of grandeur and comfort. It is just as easy to imagine spending time there oneself as it is to imagine Edith Wharton sitting in one of the vast sofas talking to Bernard Berenson, or Daisy Buchanan with Jay Gatsby (Mrs. Buchanan's house, not Mr. Gatsby's), or even Ned Lutyens having a cozy chat with Lady Sackville.

Architecturally the Phipps porch is an Ionic-order post-and-beam structure attached to an Edwardian version of a Christopher Wren house. The ceiling is roughish oak but constructed in a very intricate way and supported by beautifully finished stone columns. The floor is pale marble laid in contrasting squares. The furniture is, according to one member of the family who remembers it from many years ago, nearly exactly the way it was originally. It consists of a couple of gigantic, unmatched sofas slipcovered in chintz, a few chairs of various types, some assorted tables, and lots of plants. The whole combination was loosely assembled, and it was clearly arranged for comfort and informality, the major purpose of porch furnishing. It seems to me that the freedom with which the furniture was (and is) arranged on this gorgeous Westbury porch results from a desire to soften the rigidly architectural atmosphere of the space itself, which as a matter of fact applies to porches in general. In their hard, structural way, they need all the ad hoc tricks of pure decoration. Loosely arranged furniture is visual shorthand for an informal mood.

A similarly grand porchlike space with an equally inviting atmosphere in the midst of great architectural detail exists at Vizcaya, Burrall Hoffman's palazzo in Miami, Florida, built 1914–16. The house itself, although it sounds gauche and corny, is a pastiche of fifteenth- and sixteenth-century Italian design, and it is as beautiful as it is possible to be. Vizcaya's east porch, or loggia, is wonderful. The ceiling is vaulted and the space is open on both its long sides, facing the ocean in one direction and a courtyard in the other. The end walls lead into the house. The floor is paved with marble in an extraordinarily complex pattern of interlocking circles, better than the plaza at Lincoln Center. In the middle of this palatial space sits a heroically scaled marble-and-stone Renaissance table. Around this table and tucked in and out of the huge

This house, which lost its original porch, has been given a new one by its owners, Billy and Chessy Rayner. Their architect, Jaquelin Robertson, designed the new porch in the spirit of a 19th-century farmhouse.

plants in pots and wooden tubs are simply lots and lots of huge wicker chairs with deep seat cushions and smaller pillows stuffed in the back. The effect is perfect; it is enormously inviting, but it is unexpected, and being unexpected is probably one of the ephemeral qualities that make up chic, a word that lovers of fashion have argued about ever since it came into use in France in the 1850s. The Vizcaya porch is definitely chic. It is also nostalgic and romantic, and I suppose that these qualities are very much a part of the planning of all successful porches and terraces and gardens.

Another porch I've always loved thinking about (I saw it once years ago) is in Maine, looking through huge trees down to the water. It is part of a house with dark timbering of that curious sort that is neither Tudor nor Norman. Just dark. The porch does not attempt to be light; it is furnished with shiny black wicker of all sorts, with lacquer-red canvas covering its cushions and everything looking terrific against the dark posts and beams of the timbered structure of the porch itself. The flowers and plants are equally controlled, consisting of nothing but masses of geraniums in all sorts of terra-cotta pots, many of them covered with moss, the way pots should be.

A coat of paint can be the perfect answer to lots of porch questions, and is not a compromise either. I can recall many porches with old rocking chairs of one design, benches and tables of another, and, of course, the ubiquitous wicker of various shapes and styles, and the underlying element that held the whole thing together was the uniform paint color of the otherwise unrelated furniture. The best porch colors are dark green (the color of shutters), whites of all varieties, grays, natural tones, and black. It is not exactly a rainbow of choices but as a background color for the foliage and potted verdure of summertime and as a companion color for the architectural details of most houses, one of these colors will speak in the classical vocabulary of porch decoration. They are also colors that allow the free use of awning stripes, chintzes, and sailcloth slipcovers and the assorted mats and old rugs that end up on porch floors.

A coat of paint can be the perfect answer to lots of porch questions.

A porch that was created in recent years and that embodied all the qualities of the past that I love but which belonged to two people very interested in the present was one in the Connecticut house of John Saladino and his late wife, Virginia. The architecture of the place is Georgian and Palladian, and the porch made reference to all the periods that are combined by John Saladino's own personal style as well as all the periods that are found in the charming Georgian Revival style of so many American houses built fifty or sixty years ago. Arranged in this lovely setting of moldings and columns and pilasters were an antique marble cistern or lavabo against a wall, lead garden chairs that were already there and had been for a long time, and a modern sofa, designed by John Saladino, consisting of a very strict post-and-beam frame and made soft and comfortable by a terry-cloth-covered pad. From then on, it was pots and paths and topiary and daydreams of Derbyshire or Tuscany or the wonders of Connecticut itself as you looked to the distant hills. Whatever else they are, porches are box seats from which those of us who worship nature can relax and watch the show.

Westbury House was built on Long Island by the Phipps family in the first decade of this century. The west facade has a formal Ionic-order post-and-beam porch with a marble floor, but the assortment of comfortable sofas and chairs gives it the informality a porch should have.

GARDEN PLEASURES

Even the most hardened philistine seems to love flowers. They are what we present as tokens of our love. We wear them. We ornament our houses with them. They are fitting decorations for our most august occasions—weddings and funerals. So it is extremely rewarding to be able to grow and possess the tangible beauty of flowers.

When I was growing up in Indiana, the word *garden* meant vegetable garden to most people, and they were often beautiful. Our own garden, in a far corner of the yard, was entered from the side (I can still hear the squeak of the gate and the sound it made when it slammed shut). It was screened from the street side by irises and peonies and neat rows of tall zinnias, the Indiana state flower. Behind the flowers, low plants grew in the first rows: lettuces, cabbages, and carrots. Toward the back, the plants got taller and taller, ending up with tomatoes on stakes and great tepee affairs with lima beans trained up them. The back fence was covered with morning glories and lined with hollyhocks and the terrible enemy, honeysuckle, which my father despised. Along the side fence were the redbud and apple trees my father had planted before I was born. My view of this garden was usually from the top of the biggest apple tree, and it was lovely all summer long.

Many gardens have a less nourishing yet practical purpose: They are planned with the architecture of the house in mind, and their role is to enhance the buildings around which they are planted. This is probably the most common type of garden. It has everything to recommend it. First, there are few houses that do not benefit from landscaping of one sort or another. Second, this type of garden is readily seen from both the outside and the inside of the house and is therefore a source of constant visual pleasure.

Most of the world's grand houses stand aloof from their gardens, their architectural attributes being too lofty to permit any interference. For their inhabitants, the remote gardens of these palatial dwellings provide opportunities for distant walks full of surprises and escapes. These vast horticultural compositions seem nowadays to have a museum quality, but I adore visiting them, private ones as well as those open to the public. As a rule, you enter the imposing house through the entrance court door, which is usually on the gloomy side of the building, and you proceed to the garden on the opposite side. Often there is a lovely door or French window opening onto a terrace. Down a flight of steps embellished with stone urns or sphinxes, the tour begins. You set off to take in the winter garden with its Classical temple, the rose garden, the woodland dell, the poet's corner, and the bower of Venus. It isn't the typical garden that any of us expects to experience on a regular basis, and I hope I'm not making it sound stiff and stuffy because it is a delight that I recommend highly and take every opportunity to enjoy.

When gazing on an authentic Capability Brown landscape with its clumps of trees set here and there on rolling, grassy unfenced land, it is easy to think that God just happened to make England look that way. But in a herculean way, Brown (Lancelot was his real first name and he was born in 1716) started a revolution in garden design. The stately gardens of his day had focused on elaborate geometric patterns and Rococo parterres leading off into radiating avenues of strictly planted trees. Brown's new outlook, which imitated nature, was radical at the time, and the history of gardening was changed forever. Lawns made easy transitions into meadows and fields. Trees were grouped to create subtle vistas. Lakes and ponds became irregular in their outlines. With that style established, many landscape architects have been battling the adherents of more formal designs ever since. In truth, of course, there is room for both schools of thought.

Whether on the large Capability Brown scale or confined to a small piece of property, the garden with a natural appearance can be a beautiful complement to all sorts of houses and building sites. Irregular terrain is often the most pressing reason for naturalistic landscape planning. Rocks, streams, and rolling contours, especially when woodlands are nearby, do not necessarily demand wild-looking gardens, but at least there is the perfect opportunity to create an informal prospect that moves naturally into the adjoining landscape.

One of my favorite gardens was not naturalistic at all. It belonged to the late Rory Cameron, who became a legend in his own lifetime. In the 1940s, he purchased a villa on a steep point of land overlooking the Mediterranean in Saint-Jean-Cap-Ferrat. His little bit of southern France became a

daydream of Palladian Italy. The house was converted into a villa straight out of the Veneto, Ionic portico and all. The garden near the house consisted of terraces laid out in crisp clipped patterns of plantings that echoed the tapis de Cogolins carpets that the owner helped make famous. The color schemes were subdued, always centering around greens, shading from dusty pale tones and silvery grays to the deepest hues of the tall cypresses that led down to a pool designed to spill over its far edge as though it were running off the hillside.

When this large house was sold to Mary Wells Lawrence of advertising fame, Cameron moved into a smaller house on the property and began another garden. Also built on terraces going up the hill on one side and down to the rocks bordering the sea on the other, the new garden was a treasure trove of ideas. From the terrace, where one lunched under a vine-clad pergola, there was a view down a path bordered by square beds. In each bed grew a neatly pruned fruit tree. The trunks of the trees were whitewashed up to about three feet from the ground, something I had often seen in the Midwest but never with such style. The purpose is to keep insects from going up the trunks. Rory had also planted in the beds white calla lilies, which were in bloom in late May when my wife, Duane, and I saw it. The pale gravel path, whitewashed tree trunks, and calla lilies were marvelously chic together.

This is a wisteria-draped, natural wood pergola that I designed for Tony and Roxana Robinson which sits within the foundations of a long-vanished garden building. The area, planted with perennials, is one of the views seen from the house.

As a child, I was entranced by a garden I watched come into being. The elderly couple it belonged to introduced me, at the age of ten, to a range of architectural and decorative delights including Frank Lloyd Wright, Carl Larsson, and Mies van der Rohe. The house was the first (and probably only) flat-roofed modern structure built in the little town where I grew up, and during its construction it became the focal point of my leisure hours. The wings of this exotic U-shaped house, considered a monstrosity by most of my parents' friends, enclosed an immense mulberry tree, very messy but extraordinarily large and beautiful. I adored the whole thing—the odd house, the enclosed garden, and most of all the eccentric owners. From the moment the first brick paths were laid until I grew up and moved away, I treasured every moment spent in this garden, watching the beds fill up and mature and be changed from time to time through some new botanical fascination. It was my first taste of "outdoor rooms." It was also my first glimpse into the possibilities of courtyard gardens that look into themselves rather than out into the world.

This was the fifties, and the most noteworthy gardens of that era were the intricate, confined creations of Thomas Church in San Francisco. These gardens, primarily urban, usually contained a lot of decking. The various levels, always enticing in garden planning, were enhanced by beautiful wooden steps in differing patterns. A great monument to this era that still exists is the breathtakingly beautiful creation of Tony Duquette in Beverly Hills, California. The Duquettes have for fifty years lived a fantasy life of arts and crafts which would take several volumes to chronicle, and they are surrounded by an aura of magic and originality. Their garden, built over the years into a small but precipitous canyon site behind a trellis and topiary fence in movie star land, proves that exaggeration and high drama, if allowed by Mother Nature to grow and flourish, are totally acceptable. Chinese sculpture, trelliswork, bamboo, teahouses, stepping stones, and obelisks crop up at every turn. And there is not a blade of grass. This exotic playfulness, based on a firm understanding of plants and aesthetic principles, is, after all, what gardening is for, isn't it? Gardens do not have to conform to the practical rules of running a house. They do not have to seat twelve or include outlets for air conditioners. They simply have to grow and look beautiful.

The most exciting movement in gardening in the past century was the idea of William Robinson, Gertrude Jekyll, and their followers to recreate the old-fashioned English garden, to use their favorite description. This was a revolutionary point of view a hundred years ago. All you have to do to get an idea of just how gaudy Victorian gardening could be is to look at any flower bed composed of ageratum, dusty miller, geraniums, and marigolds, especially a bed that spells a word or contains initials.

But along came a group of high-minded, profoundly intelligent, and deeply snobbish aesthetes who scorned anything vulgar and nouveau riche (just what the Victorians seemed to hold dear). They revived the English perennial garden of borders and beds with loose natural groupings of herbs and flowers. Their gardening with its romantic associations that go all the way back to the Tudors became enormously fashionable.

Taste was also changing rapidly in America at the same time. From Victorian excess, architectural taste was moving backward to an era of Colonial or Georgian Revival style. The architects of such houses—Platt, Pope, McKim, Mead & White, and later Delano & Aldrich and David Adler (I am only naming those who have been elevated to sainthood)—did not stop designing at the front door. By 1910 many American gardens, just like English gardens, were designed in a softer, more old-fashioned style.

Georgian Revival gardens were perfectly suited to the houses they surrounded. Luckily for us, those are the houses and gardens that reappear more than any others in our history, and once again we are in a cozy Georgian/Colonial mood. English gardens are once again the topic of great interest. Seminal books from years ago are being reprinted, and long-forgotten names of gardening greats are now spoken.

The modern-day example of old-fashioned English gardening that grips more imaginations than any other is Sissinghurst in Kent, a garden created over a thirty- or forty-year period by Harold Nicholson and his wife, Vita Sackville-West. A June visit is what I most strongly recommend, although it is also fabulous in spring and fall. In June, though, it is ravishing. Sissinghurst's modest buildings are Tudor and made of a soft-red brick that changes hue in every light. The central focus is a tall tower six stories high from which Vita's study overlooked the entire garden.

The garden is large but not frustratingly so. The plan is convoluted and cunning, but one is capable of figuring it out by going around first one way and then another. Much has been said about the individual rooms in the garden at Sissinghurst. What makes them so remarkable is their successful atmosphere of self-containment, which enables the visitor to concentrate on the separate compositions. The views and vistas leading out of Vita's rooms have just the right proportions, producing a calming effect, which is exactly what you want as you move quietly from bed to bed or plant to plant.

Sissinghurst's famous white garden, for example, blots out everything else the minute you step into it. The arbor of white *Rosa longicuspis*, whether in bloom or not, is the central architectural feature forming a great baldachin

Lovely and interesting gardens require the same personal involvement that houses do.

overhead. The beds that surround it are filled with pale light-reflecting plants in silvery tones and shades of whites, which create a sense of light even on gloomy days. There are 'Iceberg' roses, lilies, foxgloves, astilbes, and even humble daisies. Clouds of baby's-breath, 'Silver Mound' artemisia, and innumerable plants whose leaves are of that color type combine with the flowering plants in a dreamy ethereal way.

Leaving the white garden, which is like leaving a separate climate zone, you find yourself moving down a narrow walk bordered on both sides by ten-foot-high yew hedges. This dark, exaggeratedly confined corridor cuts horizontally across the plan of the garden and offers a means of crossing back to the opposite side in a cool dramatic way, one of the most ingenious aspects of a skillful garden plan.

Although it sounds preposterous, gardens like Sissinghurst are good examples to follow. You can't copy great flights of stone steps with antique sculpture, unless you are very rich. Nor can you create long allées and large basins of water and three-hundred-year-old trees. But you can look to the gardens of England of the past hundred years and apply some of their basic concepts. Since they are based on old-fashioned gardens that were themselves small, they teach an important lesson in scale and enclosure. Smallness becomes a virtue. Fences and walls and hedges are critical.

What these English gardens grow also provides us with wonderful ideas. Years ago I strolled around one of the beautiful gardens at Hatfield House outside London and was struck by the mixture of roses, delphiniums, lady's-mantle, and clumps of silver-leafed plants. That plant list and the memory of those beds are still an inspiration to me while I work our little garden, which contains the same sort of mixture on a minute scale.

You have to begin with an idea and follow it with a plan. The plan of a garden is as important as that of a house, and the things you plant are like the furniture you place in your rooms. The same personal involvement that makes a house lovely and interesting is required to make a garden lovely and interesting. A continual learning process is important in both cases, and as time goes by, good houses and good gardens improve with age.

materials

BEAUTIFUL, DURABLE CHINTZ

An extravagantly curved and extremely comfortable sofa made by Albert Hadley thirty years ago is covered in a Victorian ribbon chintz printed in France. In my sister and brother-in-law's living room in Illinois the sofa is complemented by prints of Redouté roses hung on the wall with antique Napoli plates and a giltwood fragment from a Victorian room. Various other chintzes appear elsewhere in the room.

Recently I was discussing some schemes for the redecoration of a room with an English acquaintance and she hit me with one of those remarks calculated to put you immediately on the defensive. "Only Americans use chintz in grand houses," she said. "In England, chintz is strictly for cottages." My Anglophilia and its attendant affectations are a constant source of annoyance to my family; my children cringe when I say "loo" or "drawing room." Nevertheless, I am a compleat Anglophile, and it is understandable that I bridled at the chintz accusation. It was like being caught eating my salad with the fish fork, and it is really wounding when the accusation is simply wrong.

Chintz is a word of many odd connotations, some of which are negative—need one point out the epithet "chintzy"? The word itself originally meant a sort of printed Indian cotton. It is, in fact, derived from the Hindu word *chint*. In the seventeenth century, Mrs. Pepys had a study lined with it. In the eighteenth century, clothes as well as furnishings were made of chintz. By the early nineteenth century, it had gained enough status to be used in the so-called best rooms of the house. Still, to a large number of people today, chintz is a material that should be confined to bedrooms or small sitting rooms or, to people like my English friend, to cottages. Cottages, indeed! All you have to do is look at any number of great English houses to see that they are full of rooms with chintz curtains and chintz-covered furniture.

There is, for instance, a marvelous sitting room at Penshurst Place that typifies the sort of room we all mean when we talk about the English country-house style. The manor itself is fourteenth century. The room in question was gothicized in the early nineteenth century by Biagio Rebecca, and the decoration seems to have been going on ever since. The ceiling is mock Tudor. The chandelier is Louis XV, the paintings are Dutch and Italian. There is an enormous George I red-and-gold églomisé mirror, and the sofas are covered in,

With the help of Felix Harbord, Cecil Beaton decorated the drawing room of his Wiltshire house in a version of Edwardian opulence with burgundy velvet walls, white-and-gilt woodwork, and slipcovers and curtains in a rose patterned chintz. The carpet is a Savonnerie.

of all things, chintz. Castle Howard and Chatsworth are full of ravishing rooms with tremendous chintz curtains and furniture, some from the Regency period and some decorated in this century. Desmond Guinness's Leixlip Castle near Dublin has yards of chintz in practically every room. In short, chintz has been around for a long time. If it was used originally as a poor substitute for finer materials, that was long, long ago. For many years, it has been used for its own special appeal.

Part of the charm of using cotton chintz in a grand room is treating it as though it were a material of great value, trimming curtains, for example, with fringe and rosettes and cording that one might be expected to reserve for far richer materials. The effect, although appropriate to the scale and ornamentation of important rooms, is a great deal less serious than what you would achieve by using damasks and velvets and brocades, and avoiding too much seriousness leads to what many of us consider a desirable informality and

I can't think of a single period of decorating that has not provided us with its corresponding chintzes.

coziness, especially when we are decorating on a large scale. As Geoffrey Bennison once said to me, "Why not be cozy?" State rooms, for the most part, are not terribly cozy or terribly useful. The very fact that they were not used much accounts for their having survived as often as they have through history. The really interesting rooms, and the really comfortable rooms, are the ones that are lived in, and those are the rooms that wear out and are lost to us.

The London firm of Colefax & Fowler, which just celebrated its fifty-fifth anniversary, must surely be credited with some of the current enthusiasm many of us share for English glazed chintz. The genius of the English decorators of the past fifty years lay in their ability to breathe life into the rooms they decorated, rooms that were often overwhelmingly grand architecturally. Rather than return those rooms to strict interpretations of their original states, filled with Genoese velvets and heavy brocaded silks, the most brilliant and influential of the English decorators looked for inspiration to the rooms that had evolved over the years through constant use and habitation. Having refined this style of careless informality, they then dubbed it the undecorated look. The warmth and color and simplicity of chintz played a big role in the development of this style. Nancy Lancaster, John Fowler's partner after Lady Colefax retired, was quoted as saying, "In everything, you want to understate; don't do everything to the last detail. Let other people's imagination work. Many rooms have been spoiled because people don't know when to stop." The luxury of Mrs. Lancaster's rooms may not look understated to our eyes, but in fact they exude a sense of comfort and fresh color that belies their true grandeur. They are incredibly inviting, and they are understated, given their context. Chintz is one of the means used to achieve this understatement. It is very pretty, it is not intimidating, and it has a colorfulness that is always refreshing.

In over-whelmingly grand English rooms, chintz is one of the means used to achieve an inviting understatement.

Understatement can be a euphemism for simply not having enough of whatever it takes to make a thing look finished or as good as it should. But properly handled, the elusive technique of understatement in decorating enhances the offhand mood that makes a room welcoming. As a friend of mine once said, "I hate a room where the only mistake in it is me."

American decorators, like their English counterparts, have leaned on the use of chintz to accomplish a welcoming atmosphere for many decades. The stories of Elsie de Wolfe and all the chintz she used at the old Colony Club are by now legendary. Rose Cumming, whose memory still lives on in the shop that bears her name, is also remembered for the delicious hand-blocked chintzes that she recolored and carried in her shops on Madison Avenue and Park Avenue. Her house on West 53rd Street had the prettiest chintz bedroom in the world, filled with giant hollyhocks in shades of blue and mauve. Dorothy Draper made cabbage roses printed on chintz her trademark. In Ben Sonnenberg's house on Gramercy Park—a house that was an unparalleled feast for the eyes—Mrs. Draper created a screening room/party room with red flocked stripes on the walls and rose-covered chintz chairs by the dozen that made you never want to go home. Ruby Ross Wood, Marian Hall, Eleanor Brown—they all used chintz wherever and whenever they felt like it.

More recently, Sister Parish has been the torchbearer for the sort of decoration that is so deeply rooted in the traditions of grand English houses. Mrs. Parish, whose friendship with Mrs. Lancaster and Mr. Fowler goes back

An old faded chintz covers the walls of a small room with a rounded end wall in a house in Grasse that once belonged to Charles and Marie-Laure de Noailles. This room is done in the reverse of the usual manner: furniture in plain materials and walls in a print.

over forty years, was even, for a brief time after World War II, affiliated with the London firm. Her rooms with their lavish use of chintzes have had an enormous effect on an entire generation of American decorators, who have been inspired to return to the English sources for further instruction and inspiration. One of the many lessons to be learned from Mrs. Parish's rooms is that by using chintz in place of richer, more ponderous materials, you are able to use more elaborate pieces of furniture without sacrificing the desired effect of inviting warmth. Gilded furniture, which symbolizes stifling formality to many people, takes on an entirely different mood when combined with chintz. If not humble, it at least assumes a degree of modesty that makes it seem appropriate in everyday spaces.

In a funny way, the English country-house style is all a game of addition and subtraction. In a really grand room, you have to subtract in order to make it comfortable. In rooms with less important architecture, you have to add in order to arrive at that pleasant degree of richness. Whether you are

In the seventeenth century, Mrs. Pepys had a study lined with chintz.

toning down overly formidable architecture with simple furniture, or bolstering prosaic architecture with fancy furniture, the perfect leavening agent is chintz. Antique carpets, whether needlepoint or any of the large category of loomed rugs, seem fresher when there is some lighthearted chintz nearby. And, of course, the possibilities of mixing in spots of color are limitless given the broad palette that makes up most chintz colorings. Still, there are no set formulas. You can always experiment.

We have all seen rooms with one chintz slipcover in the midst of furniture covered in more sober materials, and that one casual touch breaks the seriousness of the whole scheme. In other rooms, a few such casual pieces of furniture and some pillows may be all that is required. Elsewhere, chintz can be confined to the windows, surrounding the room with a uniform pattern. Finally, the entire room can be covered in it, including the walls. Leaf through any book of designs from the Regency period and you will find the most extreme and enchanting proposals for tented or draped rooms or any number of extravagant plans for the use of chintz—not by the yard but by the mile.

In the showrooms of Brunschwig & Fils, Clarence House, Cowtan & Tout, Rose Cumming, and Lee Jofa, to name only five companies known for dealing in chintz, there are some 900 different versions, not counting colorways. It would be fun to know the grand total of all chintzes available. Within the genre, there are types and colorways to suit every mood and every need. Some are large-scale and imposing and clearly date back to loftier eras of decoration. Some are small-scale and can be used for less demanding roles, including lining curtains or covering backs of pillows or small chairs. There are designs that are eighteenth-century Rococo and Neoclassical. Victorian chintzes, typical of that endless span of time, can be Gothick, or bucolic with dogs and wild boars, or geometric, or saccharine with moss roses—the works. The influence of Chinese silks and wallpapers is constant in every period.

Occasionally, detailed brocade patterns are translated into chintz designs down to the last leaf and tendril. I cannot think of a single period of decoration that has not provided us with its corresponding chintzes. There are even Art Deco patterns that remind one of Clarice Cliff ceramics.

On top of this mountainous supply, there are additional ways to achieve certain effects. If the glaze is stiff, a criticism I sometimes hear, any place that does preshrinking can simply wash it off. This is particularly helpful if you are trying to redo part of an existing room but not all of it and do not want the new piece or pieces to stand out. Also, if the background color is too light or too sharp, a good dyer can correct that with a tea-colored dye. This, of course, also washes off the glaze. I suppose some people are still intrepid enough to do the dipping in tea themselves, if the yardage is small.

Then there is always the question of quilting, a practice I avoid. I am reminded of those Connecticut farmhouses in forties movies (Connecticut was on the back lot at MGM), with their huge bow windows, fieldstone chimneys, and white, shaggy carpets. I believe the living room was always sunken, and there were double doors everywhere with Loretta Young or Joan Crawford floating through them. Anyway, the furniture in those rooms was always puffy, quilted chintz. Perhaps for that reason, I always associate quilting with rooms that belong in make-believe country houses. (Does the Duchess of Devonshire quilt her chintz? I don't think so.) Quilted materials certainly become more bulky and less flexible.

One of the original reasons for the popularity of chintz must be the fact that it was once so economical. The prices of today's versions of chintz prevent me from characterizing it as a particularly thrifty substitute for something else. But that is the whole point. It is not a substitute. It is a wonderful, durable, beautiful material. It can be used anywhere. If the name bothers you, call it glazed printed cotton. But never accuse it of being out of place.

RICH FABRICS
FOR THE RIGHT REASONS

A Louis XVI chair of
incomparable beauty retains its
flaky gilt finish and is covered in a
blue silk brocade shot with gold
threads. The design of the brocade
is the same period as the design
of the chair—an important rule to
follow when you are covering
serious furniture. The palatial
setting in which no surface is less
rich than any other has parquet
de Versailles floors, marbleized
baseboards, and gilded
carved paneling.

For many people, the word *rich* implies an excess that is tasteless and unattractive, and they take great pains to avoid giving such an appearance. The word itself may be avoided, except when referring to gravy perhaps, and even then it is often pejorative. Nancy Mitford chided us for the substitution of the word *wealthy* when speaking of the rich; she considered it a hopelessly middle-class euphemism.

In decorating, an awful lot of people just cannot handle rich materials, which seem to them to represent gauche excess and a violation of our old-fashioned love of restraint and self-discipline. Worse still, many people use rich materials and fail, achieving results that are more reminiscent of King Farouk's palace than *The House in Good Taste* (that invaluable guide ghost-written by Ruby Ross Wood for Elsie de Wolfe).

Of course it is not unnatural for Americans to be wary of richness, but in spite of our Puritanical tradition of shunning luxurious worldly trappings, there have occurred, off and on in our history, several periods of lavish design. I suppose they always had to do (and still have to do) with strong economic factors and weak spiritual ones. Think of all those New England shipping magnates getting rich off molasses, slaves, and rum. Their houses gradually lost the characteristic plainness of their more devout forebears. All over the country, cut velvets and brocades and brocatelles and damasks were added to the decorating vocabulary of prosperous people who had previously found them too foreign and opulent to be considered appropriate. It seems that exoticness, once thought unattractive, became a positive aspect of these terribly rich materials and their uses. Turkish, Chinese, and Moroccan nooks and corners appeared from Newport to San Francisco, and by the end of the nineteenth century the variety of ornate styles in common use by architects and decorating companies is almost beyond cataloging.

Rich materials should look patrician, not nouveau riche.

The reaction to the confusing and often truly hideous richness of late Victorian decoration was characterized by conservatism and restraint, qualities that reminded us of our straitlaced past and have always had a big appeal in America. One sure sign of this restraint was the infrequency of the use of brocades and cut and voided velvets. Instead, richness was limited to a small group of materials—plain velvet (probably not silk) and the large range of damasks which can be very subtle. Then the Modern movement came along with its even more stringent view of what was allowed. The don'ts outnumbered the do's. We are, at present, going through a reaction to *that* period. When you have had it with such cheerless admonishments as "Less is more" and "Form follows function," then you probably want to turn to the more sensuous realm of silk, velvet, and brocade.

If you head off in this direction, however, you had better be careful because there is a whole history of vulgarians lurking in the shadows. Concentrate not on the complicated and often difficult-to-decipher movements of the past 125 years but on the earlier, seminal periods of architecture—periods during which architecture and decoration were totally integrated. If you study some of the still-existing William Kent interiors, you will see architectural plasterwork and furniture carving designed by the same hand. You will also see fabulous damasks and velvets, some of which are completely original. The same is true of Rococo rooms in which the paneling and the brocades used on the furniture covers were carefully related in color and design. Robert Adam's interiors incorporated carpets and fabrics that exactly repeated the motifs of his architecture. This interrelation of rich fabric to the architecture in which it was placed is enormously interesting. It also enables you to understand what was originally intended.

Another area of study that is hugely illuminating is the decoration of some of the more chaste Edwardians—Edith Wharton and Ogden Codman, Stanford White, and Elsie de Wolfe, for example. They combined American discipline with a love of richness and comfort. They also understood the fundamentals of historical styles.

We are so bombarded by trends in our time that it is sometimes difficult to figure out what is going on. There is a kind of kangaroo feeling as one jumps from the Vienna Secession to the Second Empire, or from the Bauhaus to the Biedermeier, but this nervous switching about is bound to be a more or less permanent condition because we live in an era of knowledgeable interest in correct restoration and revival. This insistence on correctness should certainly extend to fabrics and their intended uses. In all periods of decoration, there exist materials that are precious, beautiful, and, like many valuable things, long lasting.

French rooms, I would guess, are the ones that leap to most people's minds when the topic of rich fabrics comes up—whether they are centuries old or of recent vintage. After the Depression and World War II, grand decorating took off again with a bang in France. It is astonishing to me, when I pore over books of French interior decoration of twenty-five years ago, to see the extraordinarily beautiful materials that were so boldly used. One room stands out in particular and for two reasons. First, the rich materials play a singularly important role since there were (the room no longer exists) no outstanding boiseries or architectural details; and, second, because Hubert de Givenchy, whose taste is phenomenal, once said that it was one of the most beautiful rooms he had ever seen. It was designed by Georges Geffroy for the Vicomte and Vicomtesse de Bonchamps. The walls, including the deep cove molding around the top of the room, were completely upholstered in narrow-width (thirty inches or so) green silk velvet. There is nothing more luxurious than silk velvet. Unfortunately, there are few things more expensive either. At $150 a yard, and narrow width at that, it is a very extravagant material to use. In any case, the late M. Geffroy placed in front of these green velvet walls upholstered furniture covered in cognac-colored silk velvet with inserts and cushions of that marvelous French velvet (still available today) woven in a tiger pattern. The curtains were very simple with no trim and no visible poles or rings; they were merely a continuation of the walls. The room was severe and rich at the same time.

Walls covered in linen or cotton velvet, if not quite as remarkable as those covered in silk velvet, are nevertheless very beautiful too. Another important thing to consider about velvet walls is the fact that they do not show marks. A few months ago, I was in a house I decorated in 1969 and the brick-colored velvet walls in the library looked as good as new. Around the turn of the century, Stanford White was fond of covering walls with old worn silk velvet taken from palaces in Italy.

Even more extravagant than silk velvet, but more limited in its use, is the large range of brocades. Along with the astronomical cost of brocade come two bits of good news. It is very long lasting and it doesn't show spots. Therefore, it is terrific for chairs and pillows. In the eighteenth century, of course, it was used on walls, often set into panels. That taste is a little remote these days. It would also require a Croesus to afford it. But finely carved French or English or Italian chairs and setteesare marvelous covered in brocade. Something to avoid, I would suggest, is the use of splendid brocade on indifferently made furniture, especially incorrectly made reproductions. The subject of reproductions is a thorny one. For those of you who simply will not discuss them, please look the other way for a minute while I say that there are, as a matter of fact, some very good reproductions. Many of the good ones are actually quite old themselves, and some of the best ones, alas, are passed off for or honestly thought to be antiques. They must be dealt with, however, because most historically inspired decoration simply has to include some reproduction furniture. Why not do the best you can, then, and not be tricked into owning really unacceptable reproductions? Good reproduction chairs, like good antique chairs, lend themselves very well indeed to the use of rich materials.

Nothing adds greater coherence to a drawing room than a set of four or six handsome, comfortable open armchairs. Furthermore, nothing gives seating arrangements greater flexibility than a few chairs that are easily moved from one place to another. They can be strongly designed or delicate. They can be stripped, painted, or gilded (or all three). In any case, they can be covered in some gorgeous material and they will then continue to look good for a long time. It is important to remember how hard it is on a chair frame to be reupholstered. All that hammering and nailing takes its toll. You should see the regluing and reinforcing that upholsterers have to go through in the recovering of some old chair frames. Therefore, if you are interested in the long life of your good furniture, you should cover your more fragile pieces in strong materials that will last, not flimsy stuff that wears out in a couple of years. Brocade can be very strong and can last an unbelievable length of time. Sunlight is the great threat, since it not only fades silk but it rots it, and surprisingly fast too.

Another terrific place for brocade is on pillows. Actually, pillows are a perfect way to use very elaborate materials, especially fragments of antique needlework and tapestry. Be careful—it is treacherously easy to overdo it and come off looking like a fortune-teller surrounded by worn-out scraps outlined in

tassel fringe. There is also the question of pillows made of bits of old carpets—Aubusson being the favorite. Personally, I don't much like lounging on a pillow that is made of some stuff that used to be on the floor. Skirted tables are also beautiful when they are draped in brocade or damask, and they too enable you to use old materials. You can even seam them in awkward ways that would never do on upholstery but that get lost in the folds of a tablecloth. And you don't have to think about the wasteful practice of matching repeats.

There are many reasons for loving rich materials: They are often beautiful, rare, ornamental, durable, evocative of a happy past, and grand. And in the grandeur lies the danger. Rich materials should look patrician, not nouveau riche. The one threat is that of looking pretentious—the single greatest vulgarity in interior decoration is pretentiousness. Understatement is a pain in the neck sometimes, but it is a good thing to keep in mind even when you are contemplating some ravishing excess. Where rich materials are concerned, good judgment is required. Fortunately, a lot of money is required too, and that usually inspires caution.

In the San Francisco drawing room of Fritz and Lucy Jewett I covered the walls in an off-white striped silk with matching curtains. The white-and-gold George III elbow chairs—there are four of them—are done in green silk taffeta and all the other materials in the room are silks. The superb secretary is dark green lacquer decorated with several shades of gold leaf.

THE USES OF WALLPAPER

I have been decorating an 18th-century house in Tipperary for years. Although the exterior has some surviving details, those on the interior have been lost over the years and so the decoration has to work hard—a perfect case for wallpaper. This much lived-in sitting room has ceilings over thirteen feet tall; with only one window wall we had a lot of surface to enliven. The densely patterned William Morris wallpaper that we chose provides color, warmth, and decoration, and is a blending agent for a mix of furniture from many times and places as well as a clutter of pictures and personal objects.

There are lots of misconceptions about the uses of strongly patterned wallpaper that ought to be cleared up. One fear I often hear expressed is that wallpaper in a bold pattern will inevitably make a room look smaller. An equally common opinion holds that an effect of great fussiness will be the result. Probably the most widely held misconception is that patterned wallpaper provides a terrible background for paintings.

Questions that arise in the course of decorating often involve the distinction between matters of fact and matters of taste. It is a great distinction. Of course, there are loads of cases where taste wins and the appropriate answer to someone else's dogma is, to use the words of the child in the *New Yorker* cartoon, "I say it's spinach, and I say the hell with it." But there are, thank heaven, certain facts that can be proven regardless of differences in taste. One provable fact is that strongly patterned wallpaper very often makes a room look not smaller but larger. I have seen it happen time and again. Somehow the perspective and the quality of light and shade in a room are heightened by wall pattern in a way that increases the apparent volume of the space. I suppose this spatial effect is similar to what happens when you move a few pieces of furniture into an empty room. It immediately seems larger because you suddenly have a point of reference. Curiously enough, the enlarging effect of wallpaper is most pronounced in tiny rooms.

The fear of fussiness is partly a question of taste. If you are aiming for a sleek room with plain white walls, even I would not suggest the possibility of papering the walls in a large allover pattern. However, there are lots of people who love pattern and place it here and there but are afraid of covering the walls with it. Yet oftentimes the most unifying method of dealing with pattern is to be brave and use it as a background. Far from seeming spotty, such a back-

The enlarging effect of wall paper is most pronounced in tiny rooms

ground can create an atmosphere in which you can arrange both solid-color materials and other patterns in the most orderly way. You will also be able to tie together disparate elements of decoration and collecting that you love but that you find difficult to mix. Another great advantage is the opportunity wallpaper provides for strengthening the architectural mood of a room. If the existing architectural details are bland, the mood of the room becomes far more assertive with the help of a good, strong wallpaper in a definite style.

Finally, walls that are completely patterned do in fact make a marvelous background for pictures. Not wall-sized canvases by Morris Louis or Barnett Newman, perhaps, but framed easel pictures of different types and periods and sizes hang together beautifully on any number of patterned papers, and if you would like to hang drawings and prints combined with paintings, the regular design of an allover-patterned background can have a very calming effect on the variety of picture types and sizes.

The room illustrated in color is one in which many of these points are applicable. It is in an eighteenth-century house in Ireland that I worked on for many years. The exterior of the house has charming Gothic details; the interior, however, owing to nineteenth- as well as twentieth-century remodelings and a fire or two, is quite chaste. There is no plasterwork and there is no paneling. This room is a small sitting room off the main entrance hall. It has a pretty, white marble fireplace and two windows on the wall opposite the door entering the room. The ceilings are high. The furniture comes from different periods and previous homes. A Georgian mahogany pedestal desk between the windows, a pair of gilded Victorian consoles, a big Regency bull's-eye mirror, and old-fashioned upholstered furniture from Lenygon & Morant, the London firm that has been making upholstery since the early 1800s in styles that have barely changed in over a century.

With only one window wall and thirteen-and-a-half-foot ceilings, there is obviously a tremendous amount of wall space. A densely patterned wallpaper seemed to be a good idea. The one we chose is called Celandine, a design by J.H. Dearle of the William Morris circle, first printed around 1895 and still hand-blocked in shades of green, blue, mustard yellow, and rose pink (available from Arthur Sanderson & Sons in New York). The clusters of flowers, derived from millefleurs tapestries, are surrounded by a trellis of foliage composed of interlacing leaves and tendrils. The inspiration of the design— both medieval and Art Nouveau—is just as rich a mixture as the furniture in the room. Forming a background, the paper is complicated and fresh at the same time, and because it completely envelops the room in pattern, the curtains, most of the upholstery, and the carpet are all solid colors. Pillows and

The walls of the entrance hall in an American Georgian-style house in Lake Forest, Illinois, were covered with an 18th-century Chinese wallpaper that might well have appeared in such a house in colonial times. The decorator, Syrie Maugham, stayed within the period of the paper with a French table, Italian chairs, and an English mirror.

This bathroom in Nell and David
Sawyer's hundred-year-old
New York brownstone was
completely rebuilt and decorated
to be compatible with the date of
the house (although it is not,
of course, a historic restoration).
New horizontal moldings were
added and the wall between was
painted and then striped with
hand-blocked wallpaper borders
that incidentally create spaces for
a group of small watercolors.
Floor, lower wall, and tub are
white marble. The fittings
are in a design that has
continued unchanged for
at least eighty years.

walls that are completely patterned make a marvelous background for pictures.

small chairs are covered in another William Morris print—Michaelmas Daisy—a design of thyme leaves and flowers in blue and green. Other pattern is provided by a small Bessarabian carpet and some needlepoint here and there. The ceiling is white, and woodwork is glazed a soft gray with the moldings left white. Since the room is a sitting room used daily by the owner, it is full of the clutter of everyday use, and that delightful combination of books, magazines, writing paper, pots of flowers, framed photographs, and so on melts away into the general atmosphere of pattern. The pictures are equally varied. There are recent paintings of horses raised on the place. On one side of the fireplace hangs a scene of Maine by the contemporary painter Ibbie Holmquist, on the other, an anonymous Victorian landscape. This mixture of decoration and accumulation makes the room comfortable and personal.

Arranged against a plain backdrop, these elements would have been less easy to combine. Furthermore, as new things find their way into the room, on tabletops and walls, they simply take their places and fit right in. If the sofa sits on one wall in the winter and another in the summer, it makes no difference. There are no strict requirements that this spot of color stay here or that bit of pattern be there.

The types of wallpaper that afford this freedom of mixing and arranging are numerous. Chinese paper, as we all know, is full of marvelous surprises. Think of the American Embassy in London when Mr. and Mrs. Annenberg lived there and hung Gauguins and van Goghs on the glorious green Chinese paper that they put on the drawing room walls. Damask patterns, stripes, large bouquets of flowers, trompe l'oeil drapery—there's a lot of wallpaper out there. And if you are one of those people addicted to moving pictures around, nothing hides nail holes as well as an allover pattern.

Finally, to end on a practical note, wallpaper is a great advantage when your walls are in tricky condition. And it can last for decades.

TASSELS AND FRINGES, GIMPS AND CORDS

American Empire furniture once used in the White House has found a new home in a reception room at Blair House, where presidential visitors stay. Robert Jackson painted the walls in imitation of the famous Dufour wallpaper showing the monuments of Paris, substituting Washington structures. I copied the curtains from an 1830s design and they were executed by Al Rothberg in white and off-white damask. The fringe, made in Paris, is in two shades of white and two shades of blue. Cord and tassel tie-backs are attached to bronze rosettes.

The word *passementerie* is one of those French *mots justes* that you find in English dictionaries. It means decorative trimming, and tassels, rosettes, gimps, and fringes of all sorts are a few of the things that make up the large general category. Passementerie traces have been found in Egyptian tombs, and we can look at rosettes and braid in wall paintings that have survived from Pompeii. This form of ornamentation seems to have lain dormant for centuries until it reappeared in the 1400s.

The obvious place to look for all this decoration of half a millennium ago is, of course, in paintings. The works of northern as well as Italian painters from the fifteenth century show endless curtains and bed hangings and furniture covers finished off with trimmings of all sorts. Carpaccio's interior views, which are astonishing for their beauty and their appeal to twentieth-century eyes, show bed canopies with scalloped edges and little tassels hanging from each scallop, and below the canopies, coverlets trimmed with embroidered tapes and fringes. Van Eyck's beds, almost a hundred years earlier, are equally well trimmed.

In the eighteenth and nineteenth centuries, passementerie, which we know from many actual examples as well as paintings, reached heights of elaborateness and beauty that are still the standards against which we judge modern trimming. Somewhere along the way in our own century, however, ornate fringes and braids came to be associated with the kind of vulgar fussiness that was thought to be reprehensible. Most Americans over fifty grew up thinking the proper place for deep fringes and heavy braid was along the bottom edge of the curtains on the stage of a theater. Another possibility was the furniture in hotel lobbies. As far as nice decoration was concerned, elaborate trim was not in favor. If any question of historical styles was raised, many

Trims reflect style as clearly as a chair or a doorway does. This First Empire tassel made entirely of gold thread has strong, stiff lines that are related to Napoleonic uniforms and epaulets.

people would have said that ornate passementerie was Victorian in character, and better for Belle Watling than for Harriet Beecher Stowe: a little tarty, in a word. But, of course, that attitude is the result of two phenomena—one is the ever-present Puritanical streak in American thinking and the other is the modernist movement of this century which reacted so strongly against the Victorian period. Indeed, one can imagine many Americans admiring the refinements of eighteenth-century gimp and cording and tassels, but finding them appropriate only against the grand backdrops of European architecture. But as we all know, rich backgrounds and elaborate details are very popular now, and along with this increasing taste for lush decoration comes an inevitable need for the elegant passementerie that is required to finish the curtains, pillows, and furniture.

If you're going to deal with fancy trimmings, you've got to be talking about the real thing, and the real thing must be beautifully made out of beautiful materials. Wool, silk, and cotton are the fibers most often used. Slippery-looking synthetics won't do.

If you are seriously interested in using the remarkable variety of handmade trims still available, it can only help to look at what went where historically. In the eighteenth century, for instance, a great deal of attention was paid to the different types of gimp and cording that were used on the chairs of various styles. The design of the passementerie was related to the design of the chair frame and to the spirit of the material being used. Marion Morgan, the brilliant decorator who created many of America's grandest rooms during her long years at McMillen, once shuddered as she saw me casually select a Louis XVI trim for a Louis XV chair. It was embarrassing to admit that I hadn't really thought that the trim in question was invested with any particular characteristics of Louis XVI. Under her tutelage, I saw the light.

It is clear that the tassels of different periods are very different from one another. A Rococo one is full of the playful spirit of its time. One from the First Empire is as closely related to the hard, stiff lines of that period; it even looks as though it could have been plucked from one of the uniforms that became so obsessively adorned in the nineteenth century. As the bourgeoisie got richer and more numerous, the demand for lavish trimmings galloped along, and the styles became, as so many things did in the nineteenth century, more and more elaborate and heavy. To see what finally happened, take a look at something like a Turkish corner in a New York brownstone circa 1890.

There were brave souls fifty and sixty years ago who overcame the stultifying effect of turn-of-the-century excesses without giving up their beloved trims. Syrie Maugham made curtains and valances that were covered with lavish scrolls of fringe inspired by seventeenth-century upholstery. Jean-Michel Frank, one of the most inspired furniture designers of this century, used massive wool bouillon fringe that was both evocative of the past and perfectly suited to the bold scale of his furniture. This was all in the twenties and thirties. After the war, a new wave of opulence swept through England and France. Nancy Lancaster and John Fowler set out on their sentimental journey, bringing a romantic, feminine view of the eighteenth century back into fashion, and in Paris, Georges Geffroy, Madeleine Castaing, and the firm of

A silk fringe is draped and swagged in a whimsical miniature version of a full-size curtain valance.

This Rococo tassel, woven, interlaced, and braided, with elaborate hangers, is made entirely of silk in delicate pastel colors. It evokes the opulent, frivolous costumes of the period as well as the art and architecture.

Jansen, to name a few, established a new interpretation of eighteenth- and nineteenth-century decoration that was a brilliant blend of historical accuracy and up-to-the-minute chic—a sort of chic that seems to occur only in France.

I suppose that after the years of the Depression followed by the war, it is perfectly natural that things would start to get pretty fancy. Wasn't Dior's "new look" of 1947, with its yards and yards of material used for one skirt, a direct and logical reaction to years of rationing? The same thing certainly happened in French decoration. Palatial rooms are expected to have opulent decoration, but the wonderful richness of postwar French interior design extended to many rooms that were in rather typical Parisian apartments. I have, for instance, a photograph of a room done by Henri Samuel, who for about fifty years has been a major force in decoration in France, in which all the furniture is from the period of or in the style of the Régence. (I always say Régence even though it sounds mannered, because if you call it Regency it can be confused with the English Regency a hundred years later.) The fact that M. Samuel limited the furnishings to the Régence period gives the room a bolder look than if he had mixed several close periods together. It also affected the profusion of trimming details that filled the room. The curtains had stiff, pennant-shaped valances, typical of something out of a Daniel Marot engraving. The edges were completely outlined in a rather coarse, two-color trim, as were the fronts and bottoms of the curtains. The tiebacks were typical cords and tassels, made in the same colored yarn as the fringe. The upholstered walls were edged with a proper braid or galloon. The chairs were edged with a wavy fringe that was suspended from another braid over which nails had been placed at one-inch intervals. That adds up to five separate trimmings and my photograph only shows about one third of the room.

I don't mean to sound as though American decorators were unable to work in the same lavish style as European decorators, but there can be little

If you're going to deal with fancy trimmings, they must be the real thing; synthetics won't do.

doubt that our native tastes and dwellings are a little simpler. The collaboration between the legendary Jansen et Cie and Mrs. Charles Wrightsman in New York and Palm Beach and later at The Metropolitan Museum resulted in a number of interiors that set a standard for all American lovers of eighteenth-century style and twentieth-century luxury. Happily for us all, the rooms at the Metropolitan will be there for a long time, and one's enjoyment of them seems to increase as time goes on. In the Met's ravishing, robin's-egg blue room from the Palais Paar in Vienna, there are, for example, curtains of silk damask woven in the same shade of blue plus cream but with the silvery overtones that characterize that splendid material. They are trimmed with cream and blue silk fringe, with blocks of two colors, and they are held back with five pairs of tassel tiebacks per window. I remember when they went up, and they are more beautiful today than they were then.

There are at least two reasons for not using fabulous passementerie, I suppose. It is fiendishly expensive. It takes forever to make. I can't think of a third reason. The arguments in favor of using it are far more numerous. The effect of richness that passementerie gives is tremendous. Intricate trimmings made by hand also provide huge enjoyment for those of us who take pleasure in anything that is part of a long tradition of craftsmanship. From the point of view of basic design, fringes and braids and cords often define shapes and structures in a vivid way that greatly heightens one's appreciation of the design itself. And with regard to durability, a point that is particularly pertinent given the expense of custom-made trimmings, they often outlast the materials they are applied to, and their reuse is usually very easy. A few years ago, I helped to recover a sofa at The Frick Collection which had not been redone for decades. The velvet on the sofa was shot but the marvelous trimmings were still beautiful, with the result that we were able to put them right back on the new material. These are all pretty good recommendations, you must agree.

SUMMER SLIPCOVERS
AND STRAW RUGS

A room that in winter has heavy curtains, richly colored upholstery, and an intricate Oriental carpet changes mood completely with the stripping of the floor and windows and the covering of even the smallest piece of furniture with unlined, washable ticking. Straw rugs on the floor, gauzy curtains at the windows, and one simple material everywhere produce the cool, pale look one longs for in the heat of summer.

People who love interior decorating usually love clothes as well, and one of the great things about loving clothes is the seasonal ritual of change. When is velvet no longer to be worn? When can you wear a linen suit? On which day do you don a straw hat? And then there is the serious problem of furs! The whole preoccupation with form (forget the content) and how we adjust to the changing seasons is tremendously interesting in the realms of both dress and interior decoration. The summer garb of a house can be deliciously appealing, and what's more it can satisfy a wide range of desires, some of them nostalgic, some of them fashionable, and some of them connected with being spoiled and easily bored—something prairie women, for instance, could not think about. In the same way that it is refreshing to put away heavy winter woolens, getting a room ready for summer can be the source of enormous pleasure. In addition to the visual delight, there is a practical side to the routine of summer slipcovers and bare floors, namely, the fact that giving certain things a breather from wear and tear lengthens their life-span considerably. This is not to be confused, by the way, with the closing of a room in summertime. I always feel sorry for those poor men whose wives and children hie off to the seashore on the first of June and leave them in an apartment full of dust covers, bare floors, and drawn window shades. That is not what I mean by getting a room ready for warm weather.

The issue of the heat is another significant element in the history of summer décor. In the days before air conditioning, it was enormously important to invent ways not only to *be* cool but also to help make you *think* you were cool. The subconscious language of decoration is loaded with symbols that carry visual messages extending far beyond the realm of mere prettiness. Now many of us count on an unending supply of refrigerated air to keep us comfort-

The summer garb of a house can be deliciously appealing.

Here is a room that is covered in summer not just for a sense of airy coolness but for the protection of its furnishings, including the chandelier, which is swathed in a bag of the same thin muslin that makes up the loosely fitting furniture covers.

able, but the desire for a seasonal change in decoration continues to be felt. My favorite memory that involves such change is of a house in Indianapolis that was well known locally for its garden and its decoration. In April, pale pink awnings went up on the outside. In the heat of July, they were changed to green and white stripes. Very chic, I always thought.

A friend of mine who lives in a New York apartment and has no country house regards the summer as a time to transform her living room to an entirely different environment. The heavy curtains all come down and bamboo blinds are hung in place of the sheer undercurtains. The carpet is rolled up and exchanged for a much smaller straw rug, which leaves a very wide border of polished floor all around. The pleated silk lampshades are replaced by white opaque paper ones decorated with old-fashioned cutouts of leaves and flowers, and all the tabletops are cleared off, leaving space for the summer collection of white saltglaze earthenware and blanc de chine objects that are arranged in a rather spare way. Then come the slipcovers. For the last fifteen or twenty years, they have been one version or another of beige and white ticking trimmed with black piping. There are several baskets and wire cachepots that are kept filled with blooming plants. These plants provide a lot of color, and they can be anything the lady of the house chooses because there is no other

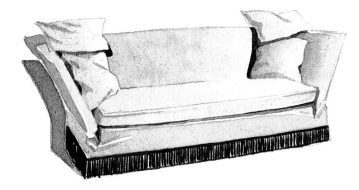

The Knole sofa with its complicated ratchet mechanism that drops the sides was not too complicated for Van Truex to slipcover in blue sailcloth dashingly trimmed with black cotton fringe.

color in the room. This kind of summer switchover is a lot of work. It also requires a good-sized storeroom or a large attic. Somewhere, a tremendous amount of stuff has to be very carefully put away. The effect is so lovely, however, that it is considered worth all the trouble. When you think about it, a lot of people go to just as much effort with their Christmas decorations, and those things don't stay in place for three and a half months.

Twenty-odd years ago, Sister Parish's drawing room on 79th Street in New York was treated in a similar way. The first time I ever saw her apartment, the large antique French carpet had been sent off for its annual bout of restoration and the floor had been given an even higher shine than usual (if that was possible). Every single piece of furniture had disappeared under beautifully detailed slipcovers, including all the little French and English chairs. It was late in the afternoon on a very hot June day and I found it fascinating to try to envision what might be under all the summer cotton. The atmosphere was so fresh and cool that it was difficult to imagine the transformation that was inevitable come the end of September.

Another room I remember from that same time was an enormous, tall drawing room in a double-width Manhattan town house that even had slipcovers for the heavy silk overcurtains and valances. At first you might have thought that the room was never used during the summer months, but the beautiful trims on these funny-looking bags that were slipped over the window hangings matched the trim on the slipcovers, making it clear that these were more than dust covers. Those who ran this household knew that such elaborate curtains and valances should certainly not be taken down and rehung every year; all that handling would be terribly hard on them. That grand room also had a chandelier, and I always thought it should have been tied up in a gauzy bag. In a scene in *September Affair*, a movie I saw years ago, Joseph Cotten and Joan Fontaine were looking for a villa to rent in Italy, and the part of the scene that I remember best is their walking into a darkened room, opening the

shutters, and seeing everything, including the chandelier, covered in white muslin. In the next scene, they had rented the house and put the room back in order, but it was never as beautiful as it had been in its cool, ghostly white.

There are, of course, dozens of ways to give a room some sort of summery mood, many of which allow you to use things you love but could otherwise never find a place for. By taking up the carpet, you can experiment with small hooked rugs or little flowery needlepoint rugs that are often too small to work in a regular scheme. Another very simple approach is to rearrange the furniture, placing stronger emphasis on being near windows and light and focusing less on the fireplace. There are obviously many rooms that do not lend themselves to this routine. However, it is often worth a try. Furthermore, if you are using slipcovers the relationship of the different materials that cover the furniture the rest of the year becomes irrelevant: you don't have to worry about getting the scheme off balance with all the pattern at one end, for example. You can de-winterize fireplaces by filling them with waxy green leaves of some description—magnolia perhaps, or rhododendron. I also love the pleated paper fans that are made to put in fireplace openings during the hot months of the year. If you are really lucky, you might even find one of the charming painted boards that were designed to block the opening completely.

Another area of summer decoration is flower arranging. White flowers look ravishing and cool in summer rooms where they might look bland in the winter. I adore the kind of simple, old-fashioned flowers that you find in buckets at the farmers' markets that spring up along the roadside after the Fourth of July. Many of these elements of summer decoration have, as a sort of natural by-product, a tone of informality that is very pleasing and that seems to convey a casual mood, as if to say, "Don't worry about your bare feet or your shirtsleeves—just come on in and make yourself comfortable."

This relaxed atmosphere is also, thank goodness, fairly economical. The whole point is to avoid a stuffy, overly rich aura of formality. That is why old wicker, either painted or varnished, can suddenly fit into a decorating scheme that would never permit it in the winter. Charming, starched organdy tie-back curtains are certainly not extravagant (though I suppose it depends on who does the ironing). In a 1954 article about the mill outside of Paris where the Duke and Duchess of Windsor spent weekends and summers, there was a photograph of a room filled with beautiful French and English furniture, and in front of each of the tall windows standing on the polished floor was a sawn-off tree trunk about three feet tall with a large clay pot of geraniums sitting on top of it. If that isn't simple, summery, and casual, I don't know what is. And that is what an open, light-filled summer room should be.

The text of this book was set in Goudy Old Style
by the Composition Department of Condé Nast Publications, Inc.
The four-color separations were done by The Color Company.
The book was printed and bound by
R. R. Donnelley and Sons.
Text paper is 80-pound Stora Matte.